BUSINESS
BATTLESHIPS

Blow your competition out of the water with marketing and sales skills that hit the target every time.

TIM RYLATT

Business Battleships

First published in 2012 by

Ecademy Press
48 St Vincent Drive, St Albans, Herts, AL1 5SJ
info@ecademy-press.com
www.ecademy-press.com

Printed and bound by Lightning Source in the UK and USA. Cover Designed by Neil Coe.

Printed on acid-free paper from managed forests.
This book is printed on demand, so no copies will be remaindered or pulped.

ISBN 978-1-908746-21-4

Acknowledgements

This book has been the culmination of a personal long term goal and could not have been completed without the significant support and guidance of my family and friends. The team support from my colleagues at ActionCOACH has also been really inspiring. Thanks to you all!

In particular, I wish to thank my wife Juliet for understanding my disappearance for many hours at a time to get the job done and for the continuous help, support and love she provides me with.

I also am extremely grateful for my team of clients, who have generously shared their honest thoughts and experiences during our coaching sessions, which in turn has allowed me to learn and develop from more than just my own experiences in life and business. They have enabled me to produce the ideas and principles contained within these pages, with which I hope to help many more people.

Finally, I would like to thank David Taylor and David Miles for 'winning the gold medal' by publishing their book *Fusion: The New Way of Marketing*; a great guide to internet and social media marketing. By treading the path first, you motivated me to keep at it and for that I am very grateful!

Praise for Business Battleships

"Business Battleships is a thought-provoking read as it endeavours to challenge the more traditional approaches to marketing.

It encourages us to change the way we think about how a sale is made. The ideas generated throughout these pages are aimed at the pragmatist who is willing to test new approaches to winning business and, ultimately, to improve their business performance."

Peter Cullum CBE

Founder of Towergate Insurance and the Centre for Entrepreneurship, Cass School of Business

"Inspiring and easy to understand – a fresh approach to sales & marketing."

David Taylor

Author of *Fusion: The new way of marketing.*

Foreword

Anyone with an interest in running a successful business will at some stage as a child have enjoyed a competitive game of 'Battleships', or at least know about the game and its idea of shooting from a position of 'best-guess'.

The title of this book is a simple recognition that this is how most business marketing and sales is done. It's not the *best* tactic, but it is the most *commonly applied* tactic during these essential tasks. This book aims to change that for you – the reader – and represents the equivalent of 'taking a sneaky peek' at the placement of your opponent's battleships on the popular board game.

It'll help you up the odds in your favour and get you more results through less effort, by gaining a better understanding of the issues that affect the buying decisions of your audience.

When I was playing the board game as a child, my brother was generous enough to remind me that taking a sneaky peek is, in fact, cheating. In my later role as a business coach, I can tell you that looking at where the opposition have placed their boats and working out how to shoot strategically from your own is a marketing 'must do'.

There's something intrinsically fun about out-thinking the opposition and finding the best and most effective way of outmanoeuvring the other companies in your battlefield of business sales.

In the following pages, we'll take a look at some new marketing and sales strategies and give you a breakdown of what makes for a winning approach.

My overall aim with this book is to take away some of the

fears and frustrations that exist in your marketing and sales world. I want to help as many business folk as possible to create real success, while enabling them to have some fun in gaining their future customers.

What makes this book a little different from most in the business advice world is that the principles and viewpoints I have applied in its pages come from both inside and outside the business world. Before becoming a businessman, I was a police officer for ten years, which taught me an awful lot about what makes people tick. Why people respond to something is influenced by a huge range of factors and how you communicate with them can have a significant impact on your likelihood of success. Within this book, I have blended the experiences I gained through policing, teaching, being a geologist and many more. Drawing together the various ideas and processes has taken a great deal of thought, but my intention was to create something different, practical and engaging. I want you to be able to read a few pages, take an idea and immediately go and use it. Having read countless books on the subject of sales, marketing and other business topics, my biggest realisation was the lack of immediate application that exists in so many. If, as I intended, you read this book and it leaves you with ideas to take away and get on with straight away, I'd love to hear from you.

Using the ideas in this book, I have built a successful, award-winning business coaching company within the franchise of ActionCOACH. Through teaching them to my clients and running seminars, I have helped hundreds of business owners from various industry sectors to step it up a notch in their own companies and teams.

In the next few chapters, you'll discover your own key marketing and sales ideas from a completely different standpoint. As a result, you'll be able to apply your own personality and individuality in business engagement, making you much more effective when contacting, meeting with, converting, and keeping new clients!

This isn't a book filled with step-by-step models, but instead I have included enough to give you the scaffolding around which to build your own strategies.

You see, models and systems are great... but most of us resort to the instruction booklet as a last-ditch effort when we've tried every other approach and not got the results we would like. Take the TV for example. How many of us have picked up a new remote control and tried to use it like the old one? I have and I bet I'm not alone!

The question is, why? If we had actually invested some time in learning the various functions and foibles of our new TV controller, we'd probably have mastered it much quicker and not ended up watching the Chinese version of X-factor whilst furiously tapping the 'undo' button and swearing loudly at the characters on screen! The point is, had we had the luxury (and amusement) of watching someone else go through this painful process, we probably would have learned from their mistake and avoided going through it ourselves altogether.

This book, I hope, will help you learn from my own and others' experiences and mistakes. It should enable you to be more effective more quickly, whilst also smiling smugly at the business owner across the street who is just picking up the remote control and a lesson in Mandarin as you turn the next page!

Contents

Chapter 1

Your marketing mindset 11

Chapter 2:

Your brain filters... 17

Chapter 3:

Breaking and entering, a professional's guide.................. 39

Chapter 4:

Making you different, Peas and PODs............................... 57

Chapter 5:

Convincing conversion... 77

Chapter 6:

The past and the present – both clients of yours 93

Chapter 7:

The cold war – brand new contacts 105

Chapter 8:

Hurrah! It worked... my leads are here... now what? 123

Chapter 9:

Have a process and bin the no-entry signs 137

Chapter 10:

Ask great questions and listen 155

Chapter 11:

Today's buyers are tank commanders 173

Chapter 12:

The art of presentation 185

CHAPTER 1

Your marketing mindset... make it a good one!

"The path to success is only trodden by feet that are led by a willing mind and by eyes that see into the distance as though it were the very next step."

Tim Rylatt

Hmmm... starting at the beginning. Seems logical, doesn't it?

I'd like you to take a different approach, if you please...

Just for a moment, I'd like you to look back on your business life. Think about the opportunities you have had in your current and previous businesses, of which the results were controlled by the decisions of another person.

What influenced them? What were the factors that fed into their brains that made them say 'yes' and as a result made you smile? Or, perhaps more often than it's comfortable to consider, what made them say 'no' so that frustration struck you low?

Take a second or two to think. If every 'no' had in fact been a 'yes', where would your business be right now? What impact would it have had on your life and the lives of the people you care about?

Where would you be living now and what would you be doing with your time? How would things be **bigger, better, different?**

It's quite a thought to take on, isn't it?

Now, I'd like you to re-join me in reality. This is where we are right now. In fact, this is where you'll only ever be. Right here, right now. Whenever and wherever that may, in actual fact, be.

So... the key point behind this thinking exercise is to provide you the basis to make **the choice**.

Choose now and choose wisely.

Decide right now whether you want to be reliant on other people to make your future, or whether you'd like to know how to affect those future decisions and have a real and positive influence over your own success.

Because ten years from now, you can re-run this 'What if' exercise and either feel ecstatic because you have made a dramatic difference, or still feel the same as you do today.

Action sections for you, the reader

This book is packed full of practical hints and tips that will empower you to develop yourself and achieve results, but... theory alone isn't going to make it happen for you.

Taking some action and actually doing something with what you learn will ensure you get the results you really want. To help you take the ideas from these pages and apply them to your own circumstance, you'll find an Action Section at the end of each chapter. These contain simple notes pages where you can write down any thoughts that occur while reading through. You'll also discover support materials that are designed to help you apply what you have read, by asking you to answer some simple questions or to complete some quick tasks. They shouldn't take long to complete and if you are disciplined enough to give them real considered thought in the context of your own marketing or sales environment, you'll really benefit!

In addition to the resources contained within the Action Section for each chapter, you'll find further support materials relating to these topics at www.businessbattleships.com.

Accessing these resources is easy – simply go to the site, register your details on your first visit and then enter the password printed at the start of the relevant Action Section to view/download the articles and materials relating to that topic. I hope you find the exercises in this book and the free online resources helpful for generating significant and long-term success!

CHAPTER 2

Your brain filters

"A moment's insight is sometimes worth a life's experience."

Oliver Wendell Holmes, Jr.

Most marketing messages that we see out there are aimed at... who?

Us presumably?

Is that really the case though?

Not always. Our brains are simply attracted to the things that are relevant to our mindset at that time. The issues, challenges, circumstances and experiences that we have had, or hope to have, are like a sieve for the information overload that swamps us each and every day. In reality, there is a massive amount of marketing and other information that simply passes us by. Our brain filters out what we don't need to see, hear, or be aware of at any given moment in time. The great thing is that by knowing this, you can actually start to use the brain's filtering process to your advantage.

In the business coaching world, we refer to this filter as the RAS (reticular activating system) and we associate it most commonly with setting goals and then being open to receiving information that supports and is relevant to those goals. The reticular activating system is actually a part of your brain and it has a simple function:

Stop overload and recognise opportunity.

Your marketing audience have the same parts to their brains as you do and it's the approach you take and how you craft your messages that defines how successful you ultimately are in garnering their attention, or not. What's on their radar at any moment depends on the situation at hand.

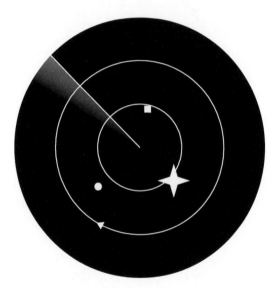

Think about it this way. Imagine you are sitting in your office/home. It's a normal day and you are taking care of some correspondence – a few emails to friends and family perhaps. You're looking for a particular address for a friend and you know that you have their business details in your address book. Your brain filtering system is now switched on and set for a range of details associated with your current aim: the colour of the book cover, the size and shape of the book, the loose end of the ribbon that serves as a page marker and the gold text on the front, as well as the likely position and page of the name and address you seek. See? It's amazing how much detail your brain has been trained to hone down on.

By contrast, at that moment in time the filters that have become so precise are also limiting the information from other sources that gain access to your conscious mind. Examples of this additional information that is being stopped might include the texture of the seat you are sitting on, the sights, sounds and smells coming in through the nearby window and all the other little details that are available to you in that moment.

Why does this matter?

It's simple… imagine for a moment your aim is to get your prospect to adjust the filters they have set right now to something rather different, when they start receiving your marketing message.

To be more specific, imagine that you are trying to sell Health and Safety Advice, but your prospect has their brain filters set for looking for that address book we mentioned earlier. The desired result of your marketing message is to adjust their brain filters so they assess the safety of the room they are sitting in, in the event of an emergency.

What kind of message would get them focused on the things you want them to be? Perhaps a simple headline that says:

'Stop whatever you are doing right now. Your building is on fire and you need to get out in less than ten seconds… what options are open to you?'

On the next page, you'll see some of the brain filters you would turn on by simply asking that question.

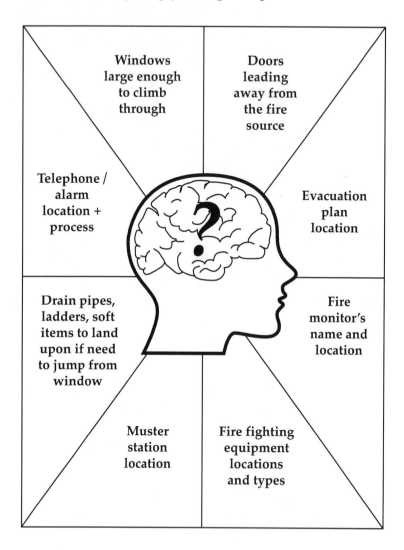

It might not be kind to mock this event up, but it illustrates that choosing the right message can result in shifting the mental parameters your audience is open to. However you do it, it needs to be impactive, driven by an emotion and effective within the first few seconds of reaching your audience.

If you're in the food retail business, a simple question such as 'Have you stopped for lunch today?' will start the reader thinking along the brain filtering channels you'd like them to. It's not yet stating how yummy your sandwiches are, or even being incredibly direct, but it's developing your prospect's awareness of their current state and the match with your offering, which in turn starts the engagement you need to make any sale.

It seems obvious – almost too obvious! But it's so important for your marketing success!

The ability to tap into your prospect's mind, and know which filters are turned on or off at any given moment in time, is the key to your winning here. If you know under which circumstance your audience's mind is open to receiving information – or, indeed, if you can switch their brain filters on for your product or service – by using effective campaigns and approaches, regardless of the situation, then guess what? You'll get more enquiries and more sales than you ever have before!

The above is a simplification of what in reality can be a challenging aim. The simplest explanation I can give of why this seemingly obvious point requires a great degree of skill is to remind you of a childhood game.

Most children at some stage during their development will have endured the painful learning experience that wooden shape puzzles present. Parents and teachers present their youngster with a box or wooden block that has assorted shapes cut into it, through which a variety of different wooden pieces can fit. A star-shaped wooden block can pass through a star-shaped hole and so on.

This puzzle is the equivalent of our prospect's brain filter, past which we have to get our marketing message. Many marketing and sales processes, however, feature more than one stage and we need to 'adjust' our marketing 'shape' as we go from stage to stage. An example might be where the first stage is a star-shaped filter, the second is a circular filter and the third is a square-shaped filter. As our marketing message progresses, it needs to change to fit those shaped filters. Later in the book we'll look at how your message can change and how your buyer's concerns can also change at various stages of the marketing and sales process. For now, a simple understanding of the concept is all we need!

Use your prospect's brain to your maximum advantage... learn how they learn!

When I completed my teacher training, I was taught a model that has served me very well in the sales training arena. I have never seen it mentioned in other marketing or sales texts and so, unless you have been a teacher yourself, it's unlikely that you will have seen it before – although it's certainly no secret!

Fundamentally, all marketing approaches have to achieve two aims: firstly, they must achieve effective message communication and secondly, they must achieve a degree of education within the target audience.

Simply put, there is no point getting everyone's attention and then failing to make use of it. If you want to really hit home runs with your marketing, don't just put your points across in your preferred ways, but present them in the various ways in which your audience needs to receive them.

This is the biggest and most common reason I see for highly technical industries missing the mark and not getting the results they deserve. Their industrial science gets in the way of their communication science. It's fine when the conversation is between two engineers, but not so great when it's between one engineer and one finance director.

Help your prospects really associate value with what you have to say by learning how they receive information, how they process it and how they then retain it to act upon it. It'll blow them away and ensure that you become the go-to choice – not just once, but every time.

The model I'm referring to here is Benjamin Bloom's Taxonomy of Learning. It sounds very technical, but the great thing is that it's really something you already know and practise every day. But it's also something you are simply too unconsciously competent to recognise, until you force your brain to divert from its usual thought patterns!

In layperson terms, Bloom identified that as humans there are three domains of learning, or three main ways in which humans accept information. He also explained that there are levels of competence within each domain that progressively show the degree of learning and the audience proficiency in a given topic.

The three domains to which Bloom makes reference are:

Cognitive – In simple terms, using thought processes and logic to learn. Solid examples of cognitive learning can be seen within mathematics, process development and similar brain-driven education.

Affective – The affective domain is the way in which we learn through our emotional experience and senses. An example of this kind of learning would be becoming upset by a given set of circumstances and the emotional journey experienced.

Psychomotor – This domain is the learning we gain through physically practising or experiencing an event or situation. A simple example here would be learning how to hold a pencil correctly and, through our co-ordination and sensation, learning how it feels to make the connection between pencil and paper.

As I said, you know this as you have been doing it for all of your life! So why focus on it now? Simple: it's hard to educate someone on how to experience an emotion by using purely factual language written in a plain and boring text format. It's equally as hard to get someone to understand the logical benefit of an accounts package through expressive modern art. It's not impossible, but it's more difficult than it needs to be!

Really thinking through how your product or service is best communicated, how your audience will become better educated about it and what is the best medium for this learning is an important part of making sure your marketing lands with a solid tap on the shoulder of their brain filters, rather than just lightly brushing its arm and being glossed over or ignored as a result.

So that's the principle. Now, let's talk through a few examples so you can take it forward and actually use it in the field of battle!

An easy example is a food-based product like cake. How do we learn whether cake is good or bad for us?

Well, there's the obvious element of taste. A marketing action that would enable the audience to learn about whether to buy or not through trialling the cake's taste would be a good option, where possible. We see this happening in patisseries and chocolate shops where there's a taster available on the counter.

This element of the marketing process is psychomotor domain. The audience gets the experience of feeling the texture, the practised experience of what it is like to actually chew and eat the item and the experience of the flavour through their taste buds. Affective learning can also be gained here, through either enjoyment or disgust for the flavour sensation it generates within them as individuals.

The second element for our cake sale might be in the communication of the manufacturing process and the ingredients involved. We could get purely cognitive here and identify all the factual data about the product, including the energy values attained and so on. This would enable our logical audience to analyse the data and rationally assess its value. Alternatively, we could include emotive language in the ingredients description, e.g. 'sumptuous dark chocolate delivering a delightful balance between bitter and sweet'.

We could also deliver a psychomotor education here by inviting prospects to become involved in the making of the product, as part of the marketing and sales process. They'd feel the textures, learn how the ingredients combine and learn through their active involvement.

As you'll be discovering here, there's a fair amount to consider when trying to make the biggest possible impact with your marketing. But I'd really encourage you to have some fun here and to give some detailed thought to what the very best way to promote and engage your audience may be.

Apple has achieved real success with their marketing by maximising the amount of psychomotor learning in their stores. The iPad is a recent example of this, which I have personally seen in action. When visiting the store, I was immediately struck by the affective learning gained through colourful imagery and the fun use of language to describe the emotional journey I'd go on through owning one of these devices. There were countless devices available for me to handle and learn in a psychomotor fashion and to use in the store as demonstration items. There was also the team member who was happy to add some cognitive learning through clear and process-driven command statements.

The really essential element here is the combination of approaches used. Some items and services are more suited to one learning domain, but the clever marketer realises that an audience will gather information and experience more easily through all domains rather than just one and goes the extra mile to make that happen.

Now that you know this about yourself and your target clients, I'd hope you are starting to think about how to strike their full learning capability and increase the education you can pack into your marketing and sales process. At the end of the day, if they understand it, like the experience and feel confident in their future use of the service or product you offer, then you're more than a little way down the sales path with them.

One other point to raise here is that you may occasionally need to adjust the learning domain that your prospect is using, to ensure they get the most from your marketing processes.

An example of this would be where your prospect is focussing on price and the logical factual issue of where they would source the purchase finance and how much they would need to do to replace it in their wallet. *You*, however, would like them to be thinking about how much fun they would have if they were to make the investment.

Take for example the sale of a puppy. The customer started

off being hyper-enthusiastic and then became cooler when discussing all the cognitive topics, such as insurance, flea treatments, house inspection visits and so on. This barrage of logic makes them recognise a potential barrier and, as such, a redirection of the learning points would be appropriate to make the sale. The classic approach here would be to put the puppy in the arms of the prospect and say: "Spend ten minutes with him now, while I go and sort something out. You can tell me how you feel about him when I get back."

By using the word 'feel' here, you can drive the learning domain back on to the affective and, as such, your prospect will be more likely to buy as their brain is focused on the emotional/affective learning involved in the task given.

Later on in the book we'll look more closely at marketing and sales language influencers. But here I'm simply identifying that the right word dropped into a conversation or marketing material, at the right moment and during the right phase, can redirect the process to your benefit.

To drive someone towards the cognitive domain, use words such as 'think', 'assess', 'analyse' and 'consider'.

To drive someone towards the affective domain, use words such as 'feel', 'stress', 'upset', 'enjoy', 'smile', 'happy' and 'relax.'

To drive someone towards the psychomotor domain, ask them about how they will 'use, do, practise, handle, function', etc., when in the real world or working environment and so on.

Benjamin Bloom was a smart cookie and you'll find a lot of information about his work on the internet and through other media. As I mentioned above, his theories are used significantly in the educational world and as marketing is really all about education, one of my top tips is to go and learn more about his theories and to use what you learn as a tool in your prospecting approach.

Taking your message to the masses and to the target groups within them

So, how do we then take this message to market? Well, the first step is to understand and segment your market. Not just *who* will buy your product or service, but also the elements that go into their decision making process. This will include where and when they will be when they are exposed to your offering and why that particular timing and delivery will appeal to their brain filters. Knowing this will give you the greatest chance of converting your prospects from just being interested, to actually acting in accordance with your marketing message.

Who is your target audience? The chances are there's more than just one! Taking a few moments to actually give this some thought is essential to achieve success. You see, the BRAIN FILTERS for each person is pretty unique, but focussing on groups of people with common concerns or circumstances means you can target these common needs and focus the attention of more than one person at a time.

So, as a starter for ten, let's look at a high street café as an example. There are many different groups that use this type of business, for a wide range of reasons. Defining the top market sectors is a good starting point for deciding who you want to aim your specific marketing messages at; for example:

Firstly, take a few minutes to create the simplest breakdown of targets possible. Secondly, define the criteria by which a prospect would be considered 'strong' within each of these segments. This will vary from business to business, but defining further who your audience is, and how their lives and businesses are likely to affect their thinking, will enable you to put more relevant, powerful and engaging messages in front of them. An example of expanding the above simple breakdown might be:

Couples living within three miles of central Doncaster, who together have a combined annual income of £100,000 or above, have no children and own their own property. The couple are co-habiting and own at least one vehicle outright.

31

As you can see, this type of definition gives you a range of factors that you can then use to reach your audience in a more tailored and personal manner. When you communicate with these individuals, you could pick all or one of the above criteria and focus your message in a way that they can relate to it more strongly.

Action Section

Visit www.businessbattleships.com and enter the username READER, with the password TARGET101 to access the online resources relevant to this chapter.

My 'hot' notes on this chapter

_____

_____

_____

_____

_____

_____

_____

_____

Actions

The brain filters I already know my prospective customers are open to, plus the ones I want to turn on through marketing, are:

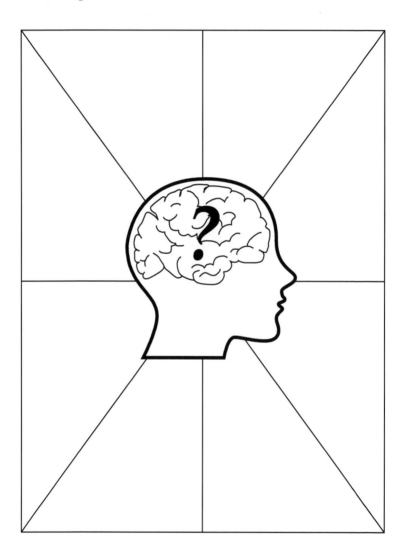

The top five questions you could ask a prospect to raise their focus on the topics in your diagram are:

1 _____

_____

_____

2 _____

_____

_____

3 _____

_____

_____

4 _____

_____

_____

5 _____

_____

_____

The top ten target markets I have / need to engage with are:

1 _____

2 _____

3 _____

4 _____

5 _____

6 _____

7 _____

8 _____

9 _____

10 _____

Two things I can do to get greater...

Cognitive interaction with my prospects
(Get them thinking facts and figures, etc... about)

1 _____

_____

2 _____

_____

Affective interaction with my prospects
(Get them experiencing an emotion about)

1 _____

_____

2 _____

_____

Psychomotor interaction with my prospects
(Get them involved in using / doing / testing / trialling)

1 _____

_____

2 _____

_____

CHAPTER 3

Breaking and entering...
A professional's guide

"...when you have eliminated the impossible, whatever remains, however improbable, must be the truth."

Sherlock Holmes
'The Sign of the Four'

During my years as a police officer, I was lucky enough to be trained in the indelicate art of breaking in the doors of our 'clients'.

It might look to the outsider as though it's simply a matter of brute force and ignorance and, in fact, in many cases that was the approach we took!

That doesn't mean it's the best approach, however, and there are some things I learned from this experience that have a real resonance with marketing and sales effectiveness in the business world.

Let me introduce you to the 'Enforcer'.

More commonly called 'The Big Red Key' by police officers, this 17-kilo lump of metal has one prime purpose: to get the door open as quickly as possible. Wielded by an expert, this is a fantastic bit of kit and can make mincemeat of most door locks in no time at all. However, when used by an untrained team, it gets the job done but with far more effort than is really necessary.

This is exactly the situation that lots of businesses experience with their marketing. They have all the tools at their disposal, but because they wield them without much expertise a lot of effort is wasted.

Q.   What's the marketing equivalent of 'The Big Red Key'?

A.   A solid recognition of the prospect's need and a message to match it with a solution!

The essential point of the answer given above is that it requires research by you!

You need to understand the buying motives of your audience by market sector and the key fears that they have about dealing with not just you, but also your industry or business type.

Find out their thinking before marketing to them and you'll get a much better result. Surveys, team discussions, researching the messages your successful competitors use in their marketing or websites, reading the magazines your target audience read, reviewing industry media (if you're B2B sales) and more, are all valid strategies.

For a high investment campaign, using an experienced market research company can pay dividends. In the modern world, using the power of analytics to assess the most common search terms and the traffic they generate can be helpful too.

For example, in the hotel industry a significant number of people who conduct an internet search using a 'local area + hotel' keyword phrase will also conduct a follow-up search using a 'TripAdvisor (or similar review site) + hotel name' keyword phrase. (TripAdvisor - www.tripadvisor.com - is a travel review site with customer experiences.)

This means that your hotel marketing should not only convey your own message, but also ensure that your satisfied customers place their positive reviews on to the review sites more frequently and more positively.

Get this right and you are not only addressing the challenge of engaging the interest of new prospects, but also covering the issues of their primary fears to do with the hotel industry in the best possible way: client testimony!

And the same is true for any industry. I could name any number of sectors and you'd be able to tell me the primary areas of concern in making a decision to engage with them.

In the age of social media, the power of entities such as Facebook, Twitter, LinkedIn, Google+, YouTube and the many others that exist is something most businesses simply cannot afford to ignore.

Making sure you have the right coverage and exposure on these entities can make or break businesses, and having a communication strategy that ensures this is now becoming a crucial part of the marketing strategy.

While the more traditional methods of marketing still have significant clout, I believe that internet marketing is likely to play an ever-increasingly important role in the success of ongoing business. The ins and outs of how to achieve social marketing greatness is not the subject of this book (it's a giant topic in its own right), but there are some very good training courses and texts out there and I would encourage you to do some learning on how this can work well for your business.

For now, I'd like to draw back to the more general context of marketing and sales and suggest that whatever medium or method you choose to match the brain filters of your potential clients, the core situation remains the same.

Having a good understanding of why your prospects will want the solution that your service or product can offer is key, but it's equally important to understand their viewpoint in that context. The reason WE feel they should want or need our product or service may be close to the mark, or a million miles away. The important question is why THEY would view themselves as needing or wanting the same product or service. Jeffrey Gitomer says it best when he states: "People buy for their reasons, not yours. Find out theirs first!"

Below are some examples of how WE or THEY might view some fairly obvious product or service categories. And while I suggest a perception, it's important to recognise that I, just like you, have a personal viewpoint on these topics that is reflected in these ideas. Yours may differ, and that of the audience to which we wish to market will likely differ further. For that reason, make sure to check over time the full range by ASKING them what their major concerns and decision-making points would be when considering purchasing any of the following:

Airlines – delays, lost luggage, safety, travel sickness.

Insurance – the small print, excess payment level, renewal being missed.

Vehicle purchase – reliability, safety, insurance costs, warranty, drivability.

Lawyer – cost, efficiency, jargon.

IT support – jargon, not understanding the invoice, interruption to service.

Let's take the example of people choosing which restaurant

to visit to illustrate how to use this knowledge to your advantage.

I'd like you to imagine you're a business owner running a nice pub restaurant that serves good quality food to a broad clientele. What do each of your target markets need to see in your offering to visit you for the very FIRST time *and* which elements are they likely to have a pre-existing fear about when considering your industry sector?

The reason I specify the FIRST time here is that this marketing principle is mainly geared towards new client engagement. Repeat business and customer loyalty strategies are a different game. These involve confirmation of past great experiences and the continual improvement from a specific starting perception that is relative to YOUR business, rather than the business sector you operate in, or the client's experience when dealing with A COMPETITOR'S business.

So, in this chapter we're looking at cold prospects, considering a first-time purchase with you.

On the next page are some fictional examples of how you might look into the concerns and blocking points that prospective clients may have, as well as a consideration of the ideal outcome they wish to achieve in spite of those concerns.

Target market	What they want	Biggest fears
Pensioners wanting to book a Sunday lunch with their family.	Ability to book ahead. Seating at one table with ample space and easy access so the family can sit together. Variety of modem and classic food explained simply on the menu to satisfy the range of tastes across the generations of family members. Quiet, sociable, clean, environment. Nice food served swiftly by a friendy person.	Loud music meaning they can't communicate well? Poor customer service? Poor quality food / lack of variety? Limited space for the guest seating? Small print on the bill? Hygiene standards?
Target market	**What they want**	**Biggest fears**
Young Man aged 18 - 30 wanting to have a few drinks on a weekend evening before visiting the local nightclubs.	Easy, regular service in the bar area. Standing room where they can congregate and avoid being in the way. Range of beers and other drinks at a base price. Modem music played loudly, but not too loudly.	Long queue for dinks? Lack of atmosphere. Too few people? High prices / fancy cocktails only? Too far to walk to the nightclubs? Fussy staff who don't allow loud conversation?

Running this exercise for ALL your target markets is a great way to define messages for each, using your own perception but also looking beyond your own limited/tunnel view.

That's the starting point, but it's far from being a one-step-to-success process. Once you know who it is that you want to reach, there are a number of other key questions that you need to consider when identifying what will help you gather the attention and action of your future client.

1) These groups of people can be reached in an efficient way... where do they commonly group together either in person, online, or viewing media?

2) Which method of communication will reach them in the most efficient and impactful way?

3) Why will they actually respond? What's the key message that will match their brain filters and which you need to choose to send?

4) What action do you want them to take?

5) How do you facilitate that action being easy for them to do and you to measure?

Bearing in mind that this book is about why people will buy from you, rather than a breakdown of every approach you may choose to take, I'd like to draw your attention back to our friend 'The Big Red Key' (the one the police use to break down doors).

You see, the main point is to wield the information you have gathered about your target audience effectively to help that 'door' open with the greatest ease, using **whichever** marketing medium you ultimately decide upon.

I mentioned earlier on that there is a skill-set used by police officers when using 'The Big Red Key' that bears relevance to the marketing world at large. Here's what I meant...

POLICE 'Breaking and Entering' 101

First step: Assess the door to find out how many locks are in place and where they are.

The equivalent step for this in your marketing approach is a good understanding of what motivates people to buy your product or service, as well as what stops them doing so. This knowledge equips you with two very important tools: the most important outcomes people want to achieve and the most common objections that hold them back.

To assess the door locks in place, the police teams physically push their hands or boots against the top, middle and bottom sections of the door to see where there is a 'flex'. Where there is an obvious movement or flex in the door, it means there is less resistance (i.e. a weak lock or no lock at all in that location).

This is similar to knowing that your specific target market, for example, doesn't have financial challenges that will limit their ability to buy from you. It doesn't mean that price isn't important, but it does mean that you need to look at overcoming other blocking points that have a more direct impact on their personal decision-making process first.

For example, maybe for this group quality of workmanship is the most common objection encountered.

Once the police have assessed the door, they then strike the areas where resistance was felt most firmly. Where resistance is felt in all three areas, the sequence 'top, bottom, middle' is used.

Top first, because it's the hardest to strike and takes the most effort to overcome in terms of lifting the heavy enforcer to reach it. Bottom next, because it will stop the door opening if not removed, but also because it isn't where the greatest power can be achieved. Finally, the centremost position, because once the other blocks have been removed, a solid strike here means the door swings open most readily.

How this relates back to the marketing world is that there is often an order of priority that we can base our marketing process around. If you have more than one stage to your engagement with a prospect, then understanding this and using it to your advantage can help you get the prize in the end.

Identify the order in which the objections typically appear and stage your marketing messages to strike and remove these sequentially throughout the process. An example of where this happens might be in a tendering process, where the primary PQQ (pre-qualification questionnaire) checks out your viability, the ITT (invitation to tender) wants to know your approach and professionalism, and the pitch at the end is designed to see you and to build faith in your team and your personal approach. The aim of each stage is distinct and while on occasion there can be some crossover, there is typically one primary area of fear for each point in the process. If you can beat each one, then your prospect will dance past them all and happily through the stages.

The final point before we move on is that any one particular group will have one primary fear that is most important to them and will need to be addressed by a unifying theme in your marketing message. Consistency in the approach through all stages is critical, to reassure your prospects that while you are making a new point in each stage, this common fear is still addressed and has not been forgotten.

This last element ensures every strike on the door has an amplified effect and the likelihood of it swinging open is enhanced throughout the whole process. The police do this in a very interesting way...

I'm sure at some point in your childhood you will have thrown a stone into a pond. You'll have seen the ripples appear around the point where the stone hit the water's surface and observed how they headed out in all directions. What this means is that our vertical impact had a horizontal effect!

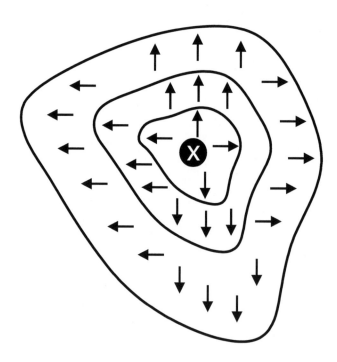

When the police strike a door horizontally with 'The Big Red Key', the shockwaves also head out like ripples on the door's surface. This 'wasted' energy plays little part in opening the door, but it doesn't need to be wasted. A simple tactic used by the team can mean this energy is not dissipated like the ripples, but in fact is added to the intended effect. It's called 'taking the spring out' and here's how it works.

One officer lies down and uses his leg to push firmly against the lower section of the door. They push hard and create a bend in the door which takes out the ability of it to 'ripple'. When the other officer then strikes the locks, the only way the majority of the force of the blow can go is horizontally through the wood and locks. It's amazing how much of a difference it makes and how much less effort needs to be employed before the door slams open.

What's the equivalent of this in our marketing message? Your USP (Unique Selling Proposition) and your guarantee. The next chapter will help you recognise yours and how you can use them to take the spring out of your own clients' doors!

Action Section

Visit www.businessbattleships.com and enter the username READER, with the password TARGET101 to access the online resources relevant to this chapter.

My 'hot' notes on this chapter

The 5 most common positive outcomes people are seeking from a product / service we offer, are:	The 5 most common excuses / reasons / objections we are given for not buying or engaging with us, are:
1	1
2	2
3	3
4	4
5	5

By understanding the reasons people WANT your product or service from THEIR viewpoint and why they most commonly WON'T engage or buy from YOU, you'll have the best starting point to improve the results you are getting now. If you have more than one main product line or revenue stream, it's worth completing this section for each of the main categories in your business, as the target audience and their reasons will differ – e.g. bedroom furniture versus carpets. Different product line = different concerns.

CHAPTER 4

Making you different –
Peas and PODs

"Never be afraid to do something new. Remember, amatures built the ark; professionals built the Titanic."

Anonymous

We all know the phrase 'as alike as two peas in a pod' and in business, for some reason, we like the comfort zone of being decidedly pea-like.

Very often during my business coaching sessions, when asking company owners what makes their offering truly different or better than that of the competition, the answer that comes back is something that is actually quite hard for a prospect to quantify.

Recent examples include a restaurant where the defining factor was 'fresh food', a hotel where it was 'friendly staff' and even a tyre specialist for whom it was 'fast service'. All of the factors that were mentioned have merit and can benefit the consumer, but none were defined in such a way that their value or why they stood out from the competition was clear enough.

If we look back a page or two at the target market sectors and the elements for which each has a strong desire or fear, it becomes much easier to identify what matters to your clients. In addition to this, using the idea of the overriding common concerns that ALL target sectors have regarding your industry, you can start to build three essential tools to help you convert more prospects into clients.

These three vital tools are:

USP: The number one differential that makes your company stand out from the crowd on a point that has real value to the audience.

PODs: A list of 'points of difference' that were the 'also-rans' for the USP. This is different from a benefit list, as it actually separates your offering on a range of factors that is directly targeted to your target market lists.

Guarantee: This generates a fear-proof vest for your prospect to put on and feel safer in. Whatever it is people worry about when selecting a company to do business with in your industry sector, the guarantee reduces the level of fear they feel when choosing you.

So, one by one, let's take a look at these key points.

The USP

It seems to me that there is a fair amount of confusion over the difference between a USP, a tagline, a benefit statement and a whole range of other terms used in the business world. I'm a simple kind of guy and I prefer to know exactly what is meant by a term before trying to create something to suit... how about you?

So to make it clear what I mean here:

Your USP is the point of difference that exists in your business that affects the highest number of both current and future clients in terms of telling them "Why you should preferentially choose us above other suppliers of a similar service or product."

There are LOADS of differences between you and the competition, but not all of them will matter to your audience. In fact, only very few of these differences will have genuine influential impact on the vast majority of your prospects. An example of this is the fact that I'm probably the only business coach you'll ever meet who has used a concrete pig instead of an enforcer to open a particularly stubborn front door. Interesting perhaps, but not a good reason to select my coaching services above those of a competitor! Perhaps the fact that I'm a published author on the topic of marketing and sales better sets me apart... or so I hope!

How to find the USP your clients will and should care about.

The filtering process to decide which particular option is most impactful can take a little time and, in fact, may change according to the market situation. The effect of the global recession has demonstrated this and I'm sure you'll have noticed that the primary point marketing messages are making has changed significantly during this unsettled time, particularly in the banking and insurance sectors.

The main question remains, however:

"Why you?"

The answer is sometimes simple to find and sometimes less easy, but if you want to know for sure that you have a USP with real intrinsic value to your target audience, test it by using a thoroughly unscientific approach!

State your USP and then have someone respond to you by simply asking:

"So what?"

If that same person keeps asking you the same question after each answer you give to it and you manage to respond five times or more, then the chances are your USP has real merit. I know… it's not exactly foolproof, but personally speaking I find this approach has a certain character that appeals to me.

I believe "So what?" is the response that goes through our prospect's mind when we mention anything different about our businesses to them. Whether in person or via marketing media, we need to know that our USP is sufficiently valid to answer that question when they ask themselves it. It needs to be clear enough, so that they can assess the value in their own way and consistently come up trumps with a value recognition.

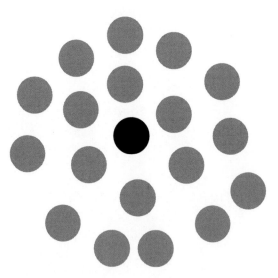

All peas are not the same!

A coaching colleague of mine works with a client who manages residential lettings for landlords and their tenants. They have a fantastic USP that really hits the right tone. Here's how this notional conversation works for their business. I hope it will help you to see the value a USP can have for the two primary target audiences here.

Landlord   "Why should I choose you to be the lettings agent who manages my property?"

Agent   *"Glad you asked! We offer something that is very different from the majority of other lettings firms. You see, one of the challenges landlords like you face is making sure that your tenants will respect the property and keep it well-maintained. The classic approach of a deposit and a detailed written home condition report at the start of the tenancy, with a review at the end, has led to some issues in the past. The deposit is there to pay for any damage, but taking court action can be a lengthy process and a real headache. Speaking to solicitors, attending court... it can all get very messy and is preferable to avoid, I'm sure you'd agree?"*

Landlord   "Absolutely."

Agent   *"Well, this is where we stand apart. Every single tenant we place will have at least two confirmed references before moving into any premises. On move-in day, they will be accompanied by one of our qualified video inventory auditors. We video each room at the site in the presence of the renter and they sign a copy of the DVD created, agreeing to the current state of maintenance. At the end of the tenancy, they watch the DVD with our auditor and any differences are noted and signed off, to assess the differences between the start and the end of the tenancy accurately. This detailed evidence has led to a significantly lower number of disputes over property condition differences and 97% of instances are resolved without argument and simply through a deposit to cover repairs. Actually, the tenants love this scheme too as it protects them against unreasonable landlord claims and, as a result, we find our renters are more satisfied and secure in the arrangement. For this reason, we have found that the take-up of empty properties that we offer is now on average 17 days faster, meaning more consistent revenue for the landlords we deal with. Sounds OK to you?"*

There it is – a decision-making difference, detailed in the space of a short conversation. The 'Why you?' question answered in detail with a real, tangible, beneficial and sufficiently different winning point to give the prospect real pause to stop and think 'Oh yes… that's for me'.

The idea is that this primary point of difference, used in your marketing message, will hit the audience consistently and clearly. The result is that your prospects will think 'Oh, they are the ones that do X, Y and Z'. It builds brand awareness, acts as a memory hook when they see your name in a sea of options and really can make a massive difference to how much business you do.

Find the USP for your own company and you'll not only start converting more prospects into clients, but your clients will also start telling their friends and families about your USP and your marketing machine will ramp up another notch. Your USP is a consistent theme that appears across all media and all client bases, with a meaningful message that speaks to your clients' hearts and ambitions.

PODS... in reality rather un-pea-like...

The USP comes as a result of exploring all your business PODs. As mentioned above, there are plenty of areas you can explore in which you differ from the opposition and, depending on the market you are trying to woo with your charms, the mix you choose to present will differ. One of the most common examples of this is whether it should be a rose, some chocolates, poetry or booze!

Taking the pub restaurant examples, the marketing approach you use for each audience will differ in both the medium used to convey it and the mix of PODs that you employ to win them over. If you don't bother to distinguish between the two audiences, you'll end up not winning too many of either group.

1) Segment your market.

2) Define the different needs, wants and fears of each group.

3) Contact each group in the most relevant format to them.

4) Follow a staged approach (where relevant) to knock out the 'door lock' potential objections early on.

I attended a sales training session recently with Bob Etherington (author of *Cold Calling for Chickens*). Bob came up with an analogy that worked very well for me and it was the difference between checkers (draughts) and chess. He identified this principle for a recruitment challenge, but it works just as well when considering your PODs.

The majority of your competitors are playing draughts. They are moving around the same piece as their perceived opponents and it's simply the layout of the pieces that determines the likelihood of winning the game or not. When it comes to your PODs, you are creating a whole new set of playing pieces, with different attributes and a different application.

If you can master the mix of playing pieces to match your clients' requirements, then it will be a case of 'here's your check... mate'. Awful joke I know, but fitting!

In your marketing mix, you want to have PODs for a range of different topics. There's lots of opportunity here and it's a matter of listing the areas in which difference can be created and recognised and from which it can be communicated.

The best people to tell you what matters most to your prospects are your clients and the customers who spoke to you but chose someone else. So get cracking with some research and then come back to the list below, to see how your own offering matches up against the top 15 listed here:

1) Ease of engagement… options on how to contact and pay
E.g. Supermarket home delivery/online shopping/ in store

2) Technological difference… faster processor, better output, etc…
E.g. Intel

3) Innovation… having a genuinely different product
E.g. Apple

4) Team difference… experience and knowledge
E.g. Saville Row Tailors

5) Service difference… consistent and obvious
E.g. Michelin star restaurants

6) Ease of location… simple convenience
E.g. Your local corner shop!

7) Quality difference… assessed by item, but quantifiable and demonstrable
E.g. Mont Blanc

8) Range difference… Simply having a bigger selection to choose from
E.g. Amazon

9) Niche difference... one of only three doing what you do!
E.g. Jurassic Park! (Fictional I know... but makes the point)

10) Speed based... faster service than elsewhere
E.g. Photo processing in five minutes

11) Limited availability difference... only a few can access this
E.g. Bugatti Veyron supercar

12) Tradition based difference... based around the process and heritage
E.g. Melton Mowbray pork pies

13) Information based difference... accesses unique information sources or offers information as an added bonus upon engagement
E.g. Specialist tax advisors

14) Security based difference... offers a higher level of confidence
E.g. Data shredding services/safety deposits

15) Extras difference... when engaging with this company, you get A, B and C as well
E.g. Magazine subscription services

As you can see, all kinds of differences can form the USP basis behind a successful company. In most cases, it's not just a case of being different, but letting others know why. This is the single biggest downfall that I see in company marketing and you wouldn't believe how prevalent it is.

Use your PODS to set yourself apart... and tell everyone!

The guarantee

Here's the rub: it doesn't matter how amazing your offering is, how many PODs you have developed or even how different your offering is if the person who receives the message has a significant fear that limits their ability to decide to move forward.

Developing a solid and meaningful guarantee is an important point for many companies in overcoming the key concerns that their clients may have.

Think of the guarantees you look for when dealing with certain industries. How many points are absolutely non-negotiable for you? It no doubt depends on what you're considering investing in, but there are times when elements of an offering are simply must-haves.

Guarantees are often an area of discomfort for business owners, many of whom are deeply suspicious of implementing the very strategy that can actually be useful in converting prospects to clients. Many times I hear business owners voice their frustration at this principle: "But if I did that, every client I had would be ripping me off!"

Firstly, let me say this: I understand your concern about the above, but typically it isn't actually a reality.

I know it can be frightening to consider putting your head above the parapet and waiting for the sniper to take his shot. But the idea here is to guarantee something that is a concern for them, but also something that you are actually confident you can deliver. In reality you are probably already close to delivering on a guarantee, but almost certainly not singing about it from the rooftops.

The idea of a guarantee, however, is that it serves both parties.

The aim?

A win-win situation.

My father relates this principle to an American second-hand auto dealer he once came across, whose motto was 'I want to sell you a lemon'. The term 'lemon' meant a sub-standard vehicle in the local lingo and the principle of wanting to sell you one was simple. He was so proud of his robust customer service model that backed up any situations in which clients were unhappy with their vehicles that he wanted to market it in an innovative fashion. I don't know how successful he became, but the idea of a salesman having such abundant confidence around his offering is very appealing to me as a consumer!

Getting the balance right is of course important and the win-win intention must always be present. But do remember that creating a toothless tiger really won't help. In other words, guarantee something that has a real fear associated with it, and not something that doesn't really carry any decision-making clout for your customers.

Find out what their key fears are and generate something that will either reduce or, if possible, remove the concern from your customer's buying decision.

Meaningful guarantees vary dramatically from industry to

industry, but in many cases the use of effective testimonials will allay the concerns that clients have about using your company for the very first time. I would encourage you to maximise the impact of these in your marketing. More on this later!

Action Section

Visit www.businessbattleships.com and enter the username READER, with the password TARGET101 to access the online resources relevant to this chapter.

My 'hot' notes on this chapter

The USP of my top five competitors is:

My current USP + POD options are:

Other areas in which our customers would like to see a company such as ours demonstrate difference could be:

_____

_____

_____

_____

The top five fears that customers dealing with companies such as ours/dealing with products or services such as the ones we provide are:

1 _____

_____

2 _____

_____

3 _____

_____

4 _____

_____

5 _____

_____

The **IDEAL** guarantee from the client's perspective would be one that would address the above fears and not be limited by the company providing the product or service. So what can you confidently guarantee to the customer **TODAY** that will reduce their level of fear and set you apart from competitors?

_____

_____

_____

_____

_____

_____

If you can't yet, what needs to change to enable you to do so in the future?

_____

_____

_____

_____

_____

CHAPTER 5

Convincing conversion

"Convincing yourself dosen't win an argument."

Robert Half

OK… You know which audience you'd like to contact and you have a message for them when you do. GREAT, that's the marketing sorted then.

Get your coat, you're done – or so many business owners would have you believe. It's not true though, is it?

We'd love it to be **THAT EASY!**

What else is there to be done, though?

Lots!

The good thing is we'll cover it all in the next few pages, but before we do, let's have a quick recap:

Target Market defined and segmented… check

PODs identified and listed… check

USP selected from PODs and clearly understood by all members of the marketing and sales team… check

Guarantee discussed and agreed upon… check

Now, on to the challenge of actually reaching your market...

'Today is a different day from yesterday.'

I'm sure you'd agree.

So why is it that so many of us are sticking our head in the sand and staunchly defending our position of only doing what worked, or indeed didn't work, yesterday?

Bad Habit

It's that simple. We are all creatures of habit. And unless you develop the discipline to challenge what you've been doing, to check it's suitable for what should be happening *now*, you'll stay still.

In fact, it'll be worse than staying still. After all, as the film *Alien* told us, 'In space no one can hear you scream'.

One thing is for sure right now. Somewhere, someone like you, doing the same sort of thing in business, is working on something different. Something new and interesting to your audience and something equally new and disturbing to your peaceful existence.

They are creeping up on your customers and have a brand new way of capturing their attention. It's your challenge to move smarter and faster to keep ahead of them and to trounce them in the message stakes when an inevitable comparison takes place.

Michael Heppell (author of *How to Be Brilliant* and *Flip It*) makes this point really well. He says, "Who's going to be running an extra five miles for the customer, whilst you are busy patting yourself on the back for having gone an extra one?"

The second really valid and important point he raises is that we are not just competing against our obvious competitors, but also against the various experiences that our clients get in other industry sectors. As Michael says, "You're in competition with Disney." Quite a challenge we are facing then, isn't it?

The archetypal trier is Wile E. Coyote, the famous and somewhat lovable cartoon character. Whilst often frustrated and rarely effective, this roguish coyote's murderous insistence and 'never say die' attitude illustrates beautifully the determination of your competitors. Your aim is to be the elusive speedy Road Runner who's always a few steps ahead. So get your running shoes on Buster and head for the gym!

Beating the competition in marketing terms doesn't just mean doing more of the same things. It means challenging the famous quote:

> *'If you always do what you've always done, you'll always get what you've always got.'*
>
> Author unknown

In many situations, the unfortunate reality is that while you sit still, everything else moves. So keeping an up-to-date, modern marketing plan and acting on it is a definite must if you want to see your situation improve and develop.

The great thing is you're already on the right path. In this book, you've been learning some new approaches and principles that will help you stand out and get a bigger hit rate when you reach those prospects. You know your audience, you know what matters to them and you know how to define your winning argument on 'Why you?' Not a bad start.

Ideas without action mean nothing, however. So I'd like to ask you something quite serious:

"Are you defending current choices and actions which are producing only average or poor results for you now, but of which you are confident those results will occur? By doing so, are you in reality preventing your ability to create something truly great but which you are as yet uncertain of that outcome, and this makes you fearful of change?"

To be successful in sales and marketing means taking some risk. It means trialling new things in the full knowledge and appreciation that not all new trials will go to plan and not all will generate a positive result.

It also means being brave. Brave enough to actually challenge your own beliefs and to stop doing things that aren't working, even though they have become ingrained habits and part of the fabric of yourself or your company.

To get some perspective on this point, we're going to take a couple of lessons from the subject of geology, and I'm willing to bet you didn't see that one coming, but it's piqued your interest nonetheless!

I find geology fascinating as it tells us the history of the planet, but the study of it is based upon a very common problem that exists in business: we very often don't see everything at once.

Scientifically analysing what is apparent on the surface, to determine what is most likely going on below the surface and out of sight, is the science of geology.

The parallel for marketing is that both involve researching, testing and measuring certain key points and a fair degree of projecting, based on the best guess you can make with the data available.

When you are taking an objective look at your company's marketing performance, what are the key figures you tend to focus on?

The number of leads generated?

The number of new sales achieved from those leads?

The number of hits your website receives?

There are literally hundreds of different points you could review, but in most cases there are only a few that really have valuable relevance when considering your future strategies. The issue I come across most often when coaching business owners on this topic is that of the hundreds of measurement options open to them, very often either none of those are being measured, or those that are aren't being measured consistently and accurately.

The action that needs to be taken first and foremost then is to find out which of the marketing strategies you have used in the past have worked for you, but for one reason or another you have stopped using.

I'm constantly amazed at the creativity our brains show, but also equally amazed at our ability to forget the valuable things that we have created and the results we actually achieved. Take a simple magazine or newspaper advert, for example. It's fascinating how many marketers became bored with an advert they had run a few times and was working well for them, so they stopped it before the next edition! The market will tell you when it's bored, because the number of responses will drop when that has happened. Ideally, you don't let it reach the stale stage. But equally, you certainly don't want to can a great advert simply because you've personally seen it too many times!

The second action point here is to review your current marketing strategies and establish which are garnering prospect interest, which aren't working well for you and which are on the plan, but not in use. Having a broad range of strategies that are used to a consistently magnetic effect is the most sure-fire way I know to generate lots of sales and new customer involvement.

The third and final point is to run a return on investment calculation for each and every marketing strategy and campaign you want to use going forward. This last point is so often the one that gets overlooked. Make sure that what you intend to do has a good chance of generating you a solid profit and know how much you are willing to invest to buy a customer of a particular type. If a strategy generates lots of leads but costs more than the return, it needs a review and a different approach to ensure profitability before being re-run.

Before taking any drastic action, remember this: the valuation on a customer is important and must take into account their likely lifetime value. You might be willing to pay £9 for a £10 transaction, but if it were £18 for a £10 transaction, you'd want to know it was going to happen more than once, wouldn't you?

Measuring a client's level of interaction with your company after their first contact with you is also important in making this assessment. Because unless you know the average number of transactions that a new client is likely to have with your organisation and the average spend for each of those transactions, then you really are just shooting in the dark.

Other essential measures for you to include are the conversion rates from stage to stage in the entire marketing and sales process.

If you're in an industry where there is a high value transaction at the end of the process, it's likely that this process has several stages to it and the conversion rate from one stage to another is critical. By knowing these stage conversion rates, you can quickly identify the areas of sales pipeline leakage and either change the process or alter the content at that point.

To give you an example of this, we'll take a look at the internet consultancy and web design industry.

Here, for example, there are a number of stages that a company may introduce, from initial contact through to a first-time sale. An example of what a marketing and sales process may look like is below. Despite the fact there are a number of stages, each one is distinct and has an individual purpose. The plan is to recognise where the process proves most and least effective, in order to advance and qualify prospects in the process as a whole.

Get that right and it becomes a faster process, with a lower drop-off rate – meaning more profit and a happier you!

By knowing the percentages between the boxes in the diagram below, a business owner will know which stages and processes to focus on first when trying to improve sales.

There are, of course, other factors that must be worked on when doing this, including the average value spend and the lifetime value of a client coming from a given lead stream. But as a basic starter it makes the point well enough.

It's no different really than the process a mechanic might follow when fixing a vehicle that won't run. They'd start with a logical point, such as assessing if the engine turns over when the ignition is turned, and then use the results at each stage to skip irrelevant topics along the process. They'd tweak the elements at each stage of going through the engine system and fix minor bits along the way, but always focus on the key issue at hand until they stumble across the main issue to fix.

The suggestion I'm making here is to follow the modern mechanic's approach of using the statistics and measuring tools available to you to avoid a trial and error approach to sales and marketing. Track each stage, record the key conversions along the way and consistently work to improve the areas that are showing a repetitive failure.

A decent CRM or sales management software program will do this for you.

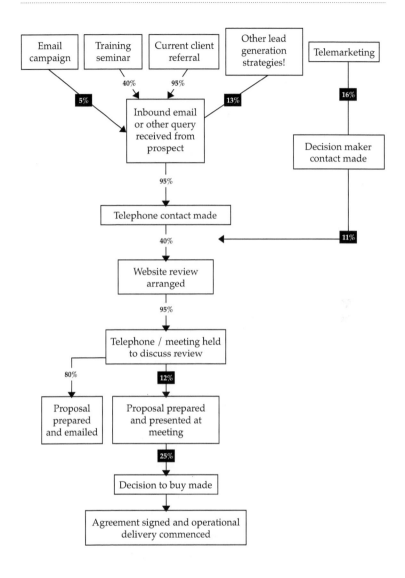

Evolution and your marketing and sales processes

As a species, we've been around a fair number of years now. And 'life' as a whole has been around on this planet for a whole lot longer – about 3.6 billion years as it happens. You'll no doubt have latched on to the subtle point that it wasn't a development race where primordial slime emerged on a Monday, and lo and behold, the IT savvy techno-geek was in place by Thursday lunchtime!

It's useful to remember that Darwin's pretext of it being a case of 'survival of the fittest' has been a long, drawn-out experience where the rate of evolution has been typically... err, well... let's put it this way... sedate would be a kind description! There are a few reasons why. Firstly, not all evolution took place in the same environment. What came out on to land in Canada has evolved to look a little different from the creatures of the Australian bush for example (think moose versus duck-billed platypus).

Your business evolution can be sped up a little, unless you like the idea of it being your great, great, great, great grandson or daughter who eventually gets it right!

The great benefit of reading books like *Business Battleships* is that, by doing so, you add another generation of moving forward into your marketing evolution. You also get this hidden but HUGE benefit: the fact that you are sentient enough and have the research tools available to actually learn from what other 'species' are doing in the marketplace. What, for example, works in the working environment of a law firm can be learned from and potentially may work just as well, or even better, in the catering industry.

We're talking cross-pollination here, people, and it might just be that principle that sets you apart and gives you the next evolutionary leap forward in your industry!

The only problem is that when evolving at a faster rate, we often feel the need to hang on to our outdated old habits too. Keeping that dusty old address book rather than updating to an all-singing, all-dancing CRM system might be a suitable example of how old habits die hard.

It's the evolutionary equivalent of keeping your appendix, despite having a whole new better system in place. It's not just a case of 'no longer fit for purpose'.

Many people around the globe, perhaps even the one reading this book, know that keeping a useless appendix is unnecessary and can actually result in some quite severe pain. I therefore suggest to you that when you move forward and find a better way, you surgically remove the old and ineffective strategies at the same time – give yourself a marketing appendectomy!

It'll buy you the time to do the things that really work and make things a lot easier.

Action Section

Visit www.businessbattleships.com and enter the username READER, with the password TARGET101 to access the online resources relevant to this chapter.

My 'hot' notes on this chapter

_____

_____

_____

_____

_____

_____

_____

_____

_____

_____

_____

_____

Checklist for your marketing process

Checkpoint	Tick or cross
I have created a list of ALL the current and past marketing methods I use/have used.	[ ]
I have rated all current and past marketing approaches for effectiveness at creating opportunities.	[ ]
I have mapped out/flowcharted each of the marketing approaches and the follow up actions required.	[ ]
For the primary marketing approaches (minimum), I am able to gauge the conversion rate for key stages of progression.	[ ]
I know which objections I receive most often at each stage of a marketing / sales process.	[ ]

If you're able to tick all five of these checkpoints, you are well on the way to deciphering the strengths and weaknesses of your current marketing position. By completing the tasks required to tick them, you'll have discovered the main stumbling blocks in the buying process and are therefore now empowered by knowing where to start work! You will also be creating a template for greater consistency in your marketing activities – one of the biggest headaches in achieving consistently great results!

The next few chapters will give you some ideas on how to move forward even more effectively.

CHAPTER 6

The past and the present – both clients of yours

"Content makes poor men rich; discontent makes rich men poor"

Benjamin Franklin

What is a client worth to you... REALLY worth to you?

If you got it right and that client came back many, many times, buying more of your offerings?

What about if they brought their families and friends to deal with you too?

And their work colleagues too...

... maybe even the associations, businesses and clubs to which they belong?

And what about if each and every one of their friends, colleagues and contacts all did exactly the same?

A great client is worth their weight in gold.

The topic at hand is one of new clients, old clients and how to generate a referral strategy that will maximise their value to you.

When you put your plan of action together for who you want to deal with, remember this: all the clients you ever need, or indeed ever can deal with, are connected to the ones you are already doing business with and the ones you have dealt with in the past.

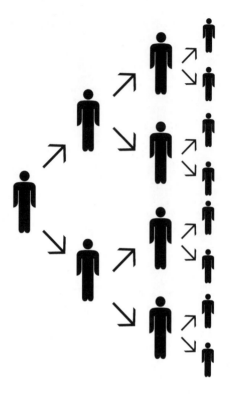

It's helpful to remember this for two reasons. Firstly, it means you start to ask the questions:

1) How can I start to get more introductions and referrals?

2) What do I offer that may match the needs of my client's contacts, as well as the client themselves?

Secondly, it means that every client takes on a greater value than the initial individual transaction they made with you. They become the cash cow of the future and the valued introducer you have always been looking for, but haven't necessarily always recognised or appreciated!

OK. So we know we've got more than one marketplace and more than one client and that we've got some old clients who need re-activating, plus some new clients who are just waiting to be introduced to us. What we don't yet have is a plan to make any of this actually happen!

About time we got one in place then I feel – don't you?

Q. Why are your long-term/repeat clients still with you?

A. Because they've found something worth staying for!

Q. What is it, in their words, that they are staying for?

A. Let's find out!

Lots of businesses get repeat business. It's great, because it makes marketing cheap! The more repeat business we get, the less new business we have to attract.

The aim is to increase the lifetime value of our clients, but to reduce the amount we have to spend to buy in new ones. So understanding WHY our customers choose to come back time and again is pretty crucial, right?

So how much effort have you put into really finding this out? If you knew with crystal clarity what it was that got clients coming to you over and over again, then this knowledge would help when you came to engage with new clients too. It would help you do something absolutely brilliant...

It would help you:

'Set your prospect's brain filters to the idea of not just buying once from you, but making you their 'go-to choice' for the foreseeable future too.'

The plan to get more referral business and more repeat business has to be based around these two points:

1) Understanding WHY current clients use you long term.

2) Reflecting this 'Why' answer forward to the new prospect/client and maximising its effectiveness.

Discovering the key points of why people use you, and putting them into the language you use and the USP you promote, will help you gain more of the same from the people that generate the referrals for you.

Help your current clients introduce you to their contacts by reminding them why they enjoy your business service or product. The same applies for past clients and I often raise a smile from my clients when I ask them:

"How many of your past customers gave you a testimonial or comment on how great you were when dealing with you?"

The answer is usually "Loads!"

The second question leads to fewer smiles: "When did you last remind them of the words they used when describing your business?"

It comes back to the 'why you buy' principle. Whose words are the most convincing to you?

"Do you trust your own opinion?"

One of the best ways to encourage repeat business is to reflect the testimonial past customers gave you back to them and use it in future communication with their contacts and potential referrals. Their language equals their value recognition and reflecting it is helpful in re-engaging past client interest.

Using strategies such as video testimonials, or written quotes from people your customers recognise, or indeed themselves, is a powerful idea and leads to more referrals and repeat business than simply re-marketing back the benefit statements that you believe should positively influence their buying decision.

Finally for this chapter, I'd like to recommend you work out a grading system for the clients you already have. This might be based on the amount of time they've been a client, the value they invest in your services, the profitability they represent, or another factor. It should help you distinguish the prized clients from the ones that are less valuable and more demanding. It should also take into account some other, less directly influencing elements, such as the number of referrals they have provided, or the fact that they assisted you through the provision of strong testimonials. Whichever gauges and criteria you choose to identify these categories, make sure they enable you to recognise where the very best of your clients are found. That way you will understand your client base and how they represent both immediate and secondary benefits to you and your organisation.

In addition, it should start to provide you with a 'tier' effect. What I mean by this is that you will be able to identify where your time and effort in client management and selection is best rewarded. This might be through the level of interaction you seek with top tier clients, or the tailoring of future marketing and sales techniques towards those clients that carry the characteristics you would like to engage with.

It's a strange truism of marketing and sales that the clients you most enjoy working with have common traits which, when identified, will enable you to repeat your success with similar individuals in the future. Going through the effort of seeking out these similarities now will empower you to seek out and benefit from a better 'client mix' later.

Action Section

Visit www.businessbattleships.com and enter the username READER, with the password TARGET101 to access the online resources relevant to this chapter.

My 'hot' notes on this chapter

Survey your current and past clients and establish the top five reasons repeat customers give you their loyalty. Ask for a testimonial/video testimonial based on ALL these points, so that you can use them in your future marketing and sales activities.

The top five reasons for securing repeat business are:

1 _____

_____

2 _____

_____

3 _____

_____

4 _____

_____

5 _____

On the next page, complete the following checklist to ensure your testimonials are able to hit/will hit the mark and contain the essential elements.

The Testimonials gathered are:	Tick
Based around one or several points of difference that you can use to show you are better than your competitors in a way that customers will genuinely care about.	[ ]
Able to be used in your marketing, because you have asked the permission of the contributing client(s).	[ ]
Confirming or supporting the USP you are putting out there.	[ ]
PROVING your guarantee or value statements.	[ ]
Emotional - i.e., they demonstrated just facts and figures, but also show the way your clients FEEL.	[ ]
Current and relevant in the marketplace where you currently operate	[ ]
Professional in appearance. Ideally, videos should be well edited and constructed. letters and written testimonials should show the provenance and date.	[ ]
Short, punchy and effective at demonstrating the client's view of your company, yourself and your product / service.	[ ]
Used within your marketing pieces to show 3rd party validation of your marketing claims.	[ ]
Distributed using the internet / social media / other leveraged means to reach the broadest possible audience.	[ ]

CHAPTER 7

The Cold War – Brand new contacts

"Real freedom is creative, proactive, and will take me into new territories. I am not free if my freedom is predicated on reacting to my past"

Kenny loggins

The main predicament facing business owners and marketers is how to answer the top five questions and then how to timeline them to maximise the impact.

1) These groups of people can be reached in an efficient way... where do they commonly group together either in person, online, or viewing media?

2) Which method of communication will reach them in the most efficient and impactful way?

3) Why will they actually respond? What's the key message that will match their brain filters and which you need to choose to send?

4) What action do you want them to take?

5) How do you facilitate that action being easy for them to do and you to measure?

It's useful to consider these questions ahead of deciding on a timeline of activities, as I have often found that getting all the answers first leads to a better plan of action than dealing with each question individually. It helps to bind a network of events and ideas together and stops that irritating habit of re-working Plan 1 so that Plan 7 could be integrated with it.

The table on the next page contains three sections of your marketing audience to whom you need to apply the questions listed on the previous page, as well as to each target market contained under each group title.

For example:

New prospects – Those you have not yet sold to, but fit the target market profile and with whom you have an opportunity to connect.

Current active clients – These should be based around your repeat business cycle. If it is a weekly consumable, have they actively purchased within the past month? If it's an annual purchase, have they bought within the past 12 months?

Past inactive clients – Those you have not sold to within a reasonable time period that is past the average 'repeat purchase' timeframe.

New Prospects	Current Active Clients	Past Inactive Clients
What has worked in the past? Why did others choose to engage / buy under similar circumstances? What has not worked in the past? Why did those prospects not engage and what can I learn from that experience to improve my chance next time?	What are they enjoying so far about my services/products that I can remind them of to re-enthuse them? Why will they consider buying it again (ongoing value) and what else do I have that could compliment their previous purchases as an up-sell/cross-sell?	What have they enjoyed in the past that they may enjoy again in the future? How has our service or offering been improved since the last time they bought and how can I communicate the value this represents for them, in order to re-start a business relationship with them?

This is the starting point for a simple marketing plan and although you may want to alter the exact details to suit your own purpose, I'm sure you're getting the gist.

You MUST know the answers to all of these key questions before making any new plans. By doing so, you ensure that no useless 'appendix' strategies are maintained and that any prior successes have an opportunity to be repeated. (The human organ, the appendix, is what is known as a vestigial organ. This means that it no longer serves a purpose, but remains part of the body only as a reminder of a prior way in which our body performed a task. An appendix strategy in business is one where the habit keeps it going, but it no longer has any beneficial outcome and therefore, really, is a waste of time and effort.)

Answering the five key questions will help build a list of options to work from. Then it's a relatively simple process of setting up an action plan and pouring that into a timeframe to work on it! I say 'relatively' because there is a bit of simple mathematics that needs to be applied to ensure your efforts are worthy of a reward.

So far in this book we've looked at identifying different market sectors, recognising their motives for buying and engaging with them effectively through strong communication of the key points. The fact remains, however, that no matter how good our message and no matter how skilled a wordsmith we are, some approaches will prove more effective than others. To add a little complication in at this stage, the level of effectiveness is different from company to company, location to location and audience to audience. The only real way of finding out what will work for you is through an approach that makes use of the maths at your fingertips.

To achieve the very best results, you must conduct extensive research before you put anything into action and make use of the experiences of those marketing to a similar audience. Simply put: don't just guess it. Gather as much information as you can, use a market research company or trial your approach on a small scale and gradually enhance it once success has been achieved.

Once you have the basic data for a given approach, you'll need to decide how much activity you want to assign to the strategy. To do this, you'll need to work out what the desired result is and then run the numbers up through the sales and marketing stages to identify how much of a given activity is required to get the results you want.

A simple way of doing this is illustrated in the diagram below. You'll need to tailor this for each proposed activity, to ensure you stand a good chance of generating a return on your investment of both time and money on a given marketing action:

10,000 flyers hand delivered to local addresses

@ 1% conversion rate

= 100 flyers actually read by target audience

@ 10% conversion rate to response

= 10 quotation enquiries generated

@ 50% conversion rate

= 5 sales generated @ average sale value of £1000

= £5000 turnover generated

- Costs of goods sold = £250/sale

= Gross profit @ £750/sale

= TOTAL £3750 gross profit generated

- Cost of flyer design = £350

- Cost of flyer distribution = £500

- Cost of other administration = £50

= TOTAL other costs = £900

= Overall profit on marketing activity = £2850

N.B. MINIMUM SALES REQUIRED FOR BREAK-EVEN = 2

This marketing break-even projection helps you to assess whether a given marketing strategy is likely to yield, based on the best data you are able to gather before even deciding to invest in it. One of the most common errors that marketing professionals and business owners alike make is to ignore the maths and go on gut instinct.

I strongly encourage you to work the numbers in reverse and consider these essentials:

What is the target profit you wish to generate?

What are the costs associated with setting up and running the marketing strategy?

What is the gross profit per unit sold?

What is the minimum number of sales that this strategy must develop in order for it to cover the basic costs?

What level of activity is required at each stage and each conversion rate in the process to achieve the right result?

If this marketing strategy will not yield a profit on the first sale, what is the expected repeat order percentage and projected lifetime value of each client generated? Will this lead in the longer term to a yield and is there sufficient operating cash available to the business to cash flow this strategy?

All these basic but essential questions must be answered before you decide to go ahead with a marketing strategy. Less exciting than leaping without looking, but infinitely safer!

Moving with the times

In the modern world we live in, it's important to remember the power of the internet and to ensure you're using it to reach your own target audiences. Matching your online marketing to the questions they are likely to ask will help to ensure the audience you seek to engage with is, in fact, the one you reach.

You see, the questions you or I type into the online search engines are the means by which we find the information we ultimately seek. The same is true for your target audience and a good knowledge of HOW they will go about asking those questions when considering your product or service is essential in building an effective online marketing mix. Seek out the services of an expert in this field to ensure you are well-represented in the biggest marketplace the world has ever had.

Even if your planned marketing activities will not primarily be web-based, it's highly likely that your target market will at some stage conduct some research or comparison checking online, to verify their decision to deal with you. Therefore, making sure what they are looking for can be found on the internet can bolster your credibility to those researchers.

Earlier on in this book, I mentioned the importance of testimonial evidence when overcoming the fears of your prospects. The web offers a fantastic platform for maximising this conversion tool and with sites such as LinkedIn, YouTube and others allowing for easy referencing, it would be unwise to ignore these websites where, if used well, you can make a solid and consistent impact. Personally speaking, I have found the use of video testimonials to be extremely beneficial and believe there are very few arguments on why to use a service more compelling than the committed argument from a previous client. After all, as Allan Pease (Author of *Questions Are the Answers*) puts it, 'If I say it, they'll raise an objection, but if they say it, it must be true'. In this example, the distinction between 'I' and 'they' is the distinction between being on the salesperson side of the business battleships board and on the buyer side.

Taking this idea one step further, video testimonials are a great way to engage the 'equivalent mindset' principle. This means putting your prospect's thinking process into the metaphorical shoes of a person to whom they can relate and therefore with whom they are likely to have a comparable thinking pattern. It's a reassurance really, because it matches with the manner in which many people learn.

There are many different sociological and psychological models for how we go about learning, but one that has stuck with me since my time as a police training officer is that proposed by two respected psychologists – Peter Honey and Alan Mumford (1982). Their principal idea of four styles of learning (shortened substantially here) is as follows:

Activists: People who get stuck in positively and learn through trial and error, without too much consideration of the potential risks ahead of engagement. An example of an activist is a skydiver who jumps out of the plane, but has not necessarily checked the contents of their backpack!

Reflectors: People who like to review the situation experienced by others before having a go themselves.

Pragmatists: People who like to weigh up the benefits and risks of a particular action and will predominantly only act when a tangible benefit is identifiable.

Theorists: People who will consider all potential results, both good and bad, along with all the potential routes to achieving them. Typically prefer the tack of research rather than action.

Understanding this very basic premise of how people engage with learning can be very helpful when considering how best to market to particular audiences and how, ultimately, to sell to them.

Normally this model is used in the teaching profession to help educators engage with their audience and to balance the educational materials and approaches they use when delivering lessons. I used it myself as a trainer and only recently recognised the impact it had on how I presented my own marketing and sales processes.

On reflection (although more naturally a pragmatist!), I found that it had a profound impact on the effectiveness of my own marketing and sales results, which is why I introduced the link to it here.

Now I will refer to my comment above – that video testimonials match the way people learn. My take on why this is the case is that, irrespective of your personal learning style, material presented in this way and evidenced through the words of others can have a significant effect on your target audience, to make that all-important decision to engage with your sales process. Here's how I see that happening.

For the activist, it encourages them to gain just enough information to want to take action and get involved at an early stage. The desired response is that they will simply pick up the phone and place an order based on the information they receive.

For the reflector, it shows the experience of others and can overcome that need to 'try before you buy'. This revokes their internal desire to 'wait until I've seen it close to home' before committing.

For the pragmatist, it demonstrates results obtained elsewhere and can overcome the need to assess on a more directly personal example. It shows the value and potential in a tangible and confidence-building context, where they can relate their circumstance to the example on the video and gain reassurance by doing so.

For the theorist, it allows them to explore the experiences of others and the various approaches and results they obtained, while encouraging action to explore the opportunity further for themselves. The chance to test and validate their ideas is enticing.

These teaching principles are really useful in marketing and sales and if you want to master the art of gaining your prospect's business, firstly it's essential to master the art of imparting information to them effectively. Picking up a good book on how people learn is the first step to success in the education of marketing, so give it a go!

*'Most people don't plan to fail,
they just fail to plan.'*

John L Beckley

I love this quote, as it really reminds me that the essence of winning in any game is the balance between the strategy employed and the enactment of the elements within it being performed well and on time.

In the pages you have just read are some fairly straightforward hints and tips on how to identify the people you want to entice to buy from you, how to get them to program their minds to do just that and an idea or two on how to enhance their learning experience, relative to your product or service. What remains is a practical guide to building your plan, so that you'll actually 'do' what you 'know'.

It's no great secret that generals plan their military manoeuvres ahead of engagement with the enemy, wherever possible. In reality, this has been happening for thousands of years and any changes that have been observed over the years have been based on the tools at their disposal and the scale of the conflict they were planning.

Marketing has also been around for thousands of years and the same changes have been seen in the approaches adopted over time. Why mention it now? Well, that's an easy one to answer. We have technology at our disposal now that means we really should be able to manage a much bigger and more strategic approach than was possible when we were sending messages by carrier pigeon!

Whichever approach you use, a plan and a process is important, and (like the flowchart on P.45) each approach you use should have a structure to it. Modern CRM software enables you to program timelines and processes into your computer and, as a result, get the necessary reminders to be compliant and consistent in your approach. In my experience, for those companies and teams that engaged with these systems in a functional and regular manner, the results were typically much better than for those who relied on memory and carrier pigeons!

To develop a solid marketing approach, you need to define three things:

1) The answers to the five questions, for each target audience you want to engage with.

2) The range of strategies you believe will be the most effective in reaching and communicating your message effectively to each group – and more importantly, which one you are going to implement, test and measure for effectiveness and then refine as a starting point. Use a break-even calculation for each to be confident.

3) The timeline for each activity within each process, which matches with available staffing power and the technology required. Getting one marketing strategy working well, and then adding one more at a time, is (generally) a better approach than trying to launch a large campaign of ten poorly-considered and rushed-through strategies all at once.

The fourth of these three essential things (☺) is to ensure that your timeline of activity includes review points to reflect on your success, so you can weed out your ineffective strategies and cultivate the ones that are really starting to grow.

This final point is probably the most important, as it seems to be very common amongst business owners to write a marketing plan, maybe even use it, and then never revise or re-write one after that.

Time and tide wait for no man and neither will the marketing changes that are going on in our technologically-driven world. Keep current, keep adapting and remember Darwin's point about evolution being about fitness and adaptability to circumstance.

Action Section

Visit www.businessbattleships.com and enter the username READER, with the password TARGET101 to access the online resources relevant to this chapter.

My 'hot' notes on this chapter

_____

_____

_____

_____

_____

_____

_____

_____

_____

_____

_____

_____

Essential Questions	Answers
The target profit for this marketing activity is (total if for a 'one off event' activity OR per week, month, etc... if for an ongoing activity)	
The average gross margin that can be achieved th rough the sales mic of items / services to be promoted is...	
The additional business costs to be borne as a result of this form of marketing/ selling per day, week, month or year are...	
Based on the average transaction value to be achieved, how many sales need to occur to break even?	
Based on the average transaction value to be achieved, how many sales need to occur for the desired level of profitability?	

While these questions are fairly non-specific, as each marketing/promotion activity will differ in its exact detail, knowing what it would take to achieve profit is absolutely critical. You can add the specifics of your activity to the above questions, but be confident of what needs to be achieved before getting started on the activity itself. You'll have better targets and save a lot of money if you do.

CHAPTER 8

Hurrah! It worked... my leads are here... NOW WHAT?

"Change starts when someone sees the next step."

William Drayton

Don't panic! You've put the groundwork in place. Your prospects know who you are and, more importantly, they have had a good reason to make contact with you.

Where you go from here depends a little on the circumstance you are faced with. However, to cover all the bases, I'm going to assume that we're selling something of pretty high value and that the buyer would require a good degree of certainty before parting with their hard-earned cash.

Firstly, a high-value sale requires a high-value relationship with a matching level of trust... but you can't ever say "Trust me."

Secondly, the buyer will choose to buy on their own reasoning and all you can do is help to guide them within that. Try and impose your thoughts and opinions on them and you'll get the same reaction as my mother did when she told me as a child not to have an ice cream, but to have a piece of fruit instead as it would be better for me. You don't want that response!

The essentials of sales:

- Have a process; bin the no-entry signs

- Ask GREAT questions and LISTEN

- Know the likely answers, but don't tell them... let them tell you! (this gives them ownership)

- Identify the process staging points and be in control

- Maintain contact afterwards and deliver above and beyond

- Gather testimony and run the gap analysis

- Re-market and up-sell/re-sell

- Build a client base that pays you for life through their level of engagement, trust and loyalty

That's it. No rocket science, just a simple series of points that, if done well and delivered consistently, will mean that prospects who have engaged with you through your marketing will continue to engage right past the point of sale and into the repeat buying process.

Take a thorough look at how these points relate to you and identify the elements you can employ to get the great results you want from your new prospects, as well as maximising the potential of your past and current clients.

Before you head off though, I'd like to help you recognise something you will have seen, but not necessarily have understood the underlying brilliance of, in many legal dramas and real-world court cases.

Designing the case for the prosecution is all about understanding the case for the defence.

As an ex-police officer, I have on many occasions been amazed at how a prosecution case could fall flat on its face because of the smallest details. It's a sad fact (or perhaps a fair one!) that many people who are guilty of a crime escape the justice wheel, based on the work of a well-organised and meticulous lawyer's approach. The policeman inside me experiences this as an annoyance, but in reality I do recognise the importance of being absolutely certain. This does not mean, however, that the defensive lawyers always hold the upper hand.

As a trainer for the States of Guernsey Police, I had an important role in ensuring that the officers placing statements before the law courts had written them in a way that was evidentially sound, well-presented and detailed enough to give the very best chance of a successful prosecution, where evidence existed of criminality. One of the most important lessons I learned when training others to do this effectively was that the devil really is in the detail. On many occasions, the case for the prosecution was not only supported by what had been directly witnessed, but also by detailing other observations that countered the potential defences.

A simple example of this is where an individual has been involved in an assault. The statement obtained from the victim must not only contain the evidence of the force that was received and the resulting injury, but must also contain any other detail that counters the potential defensive arguments of:

Self defence

Victim credibility (i.e. sobriety, eyesight, maintenance of consciousness)

Lawful sport

Lawful chastisement

Defence of another person

Defence of own or another's property

... and no doubt a few that, over time, I have forgotten!

The same issue arises when you are planning your case for the prosecution in your marketing and sales media and scripts.

You and I already know that not everyone buys everything that a salesperson offers them. They don't buy everything from me, and they won't buy everything from you, but it doesn't mean we can't come prepared to counter the common objections we receive, or that we can't be ready to hold our own in the courtroom of marketing and sales!

Giving a lot of thought to the principal objections that you know will be raised, and then researching others from prospects, experience, past customers and past non-buying customers, will give you a really good competitive edge to use in your future sales career.

The most successful salespeople I know don't just wait for the objections to be raised and then handle them (although I would say having a series of good handling scripts is essential for when that does happen).

No. The most successful salespeople I know are like the police officers I trained in writing statements. They are proactive and use pre-objection handling approaches to remove the objection before it even arises!

What's fantastic here is that most objections are only really difficult to deal with when they are raised as an objection. If you are able to reassure, demonstrate the counterpoint, or otherwise address the topic before that hand-raising moment, you'll be substantially more successful.

So let's get Escar'going...

The way I like to look at this principle is to use the analogy of a snail slowly creeping his way towards a lettuce leaf on a greenhouse windowpane. All the time he's moving, he has his eyes on the prize he wants. He's focused and pretty keen on lunch!

As the salesperson for that lettuce leaf, you need to give him lots of reasons to keep looking forward only. The temptation for him will be to look all around as he goes and, like our typical customer, he's been trained from birth to be aware of the potential risks from other areas.

Imagine you're the salesperson here... your pre-objection handlers might include:

"Don't worry about what's behind you, I've already checked it out and there aren't any birds to be seen."

"No need to look left; the tomatoes have already been eaten."

And:

"No need to look right; the last snail who looked right found it wasn't worth the effort and it meant his lettuce leaf was gone by the time he looked ahead again."

A silly story I know, but the point remains: what will it take in terms of pre-objection handlers to stop your potential customers from halting, delaying and raising lots of points of contention? Find the answers to those problems and your foresight will put the right reassuring answers directly in front of them. As a result, rather than being distracting, those issues become the waypoints they happily pass by without batting an eyelid, on the way to their metaphorical lettuce leaf.

In the real world, it's likely your prospects will raise some unforeseen objections, so get ready to handle them when they come about. Even the best plans and forward thinking will not cancel out or counter all the objections your prospects may have to the offering you put in front of them.

Here's how to handle a sales objection:

Buying a product or service is like gambling. And as all successful gamblers know, you must assess the game and work out all the potential before placing your bid.

As a buyer yourself, you'll recognise the tendency to look at all the options and assess the risks of any purchase you might make. But you'll also know that it's not much fun to sit and watch everyone else play all day while never having a go yourself. Remember, they want to buy but also want to be sure they are making the right decision.

As the salesperson, being able to manage confidently and professionally any objection that is raised, really well, is critical. When a prospect points out a risk they see in doing business, you mustn't tell them they are wrong to perceive that risk, or that they are in any way wrong to be thinking that way. The moment you choose to 'argue' with them and try to prove there is no risk is the moment the player leaves the game and goes elsewhere to seek their win. They need to see that risk diminish for themselves and only very rarely will they simply defer to your perception over their own.

One really effective way to handle an objection is what I refer to as the **D.I.C.E.** method. Your aim here is to encourage your prospect to review their current decision or viewpoint openly.

Here's how you can ensure they do just that.

The D.I.C.E Method for handling sales objections

D = Demonstrate you have listened to their objection and remember it's not a personal objection to you (most of the time!). Explore exactly what they mean, by using open questions to obtain all the detail you can around their concern and what they are basing their view on. Reflect your understanding back to them to confirm that you have understood it correctly – and here's the key point: tell them that **they are right** to consider X issue as important. This negates their fear (usually based on prior experience with other salespeople) that you are going to argue with them.

I = Identify whether this objection is the sole point that is affecting their decision on whether to buy or not, or if there are further points they also need to be more confident about. If it's the only point, that's easy. If there are more, make sure you get all of these points out on the table by communicating openly with your prospect and encouraging them to share all the things that they would need resolved in order to continue. In the real world, rarely is the first objection the real one, or the only one. So ask them to be honest, as you really do want to know how to help them best.

C = Create a safe forum to discuss those points in more detail and refer the prospect to the outcomes they want to achieve through the purchase of 'something'. Confirm the result they would like from the item they are seeking and then use your USPs, guarantees and benefit statements to match the offering you have to the result they wish to achieve. In particular, focus on the primary area of concern and then ask if the detail provided, or the explanation given, addresses their concern on that specific point. If so...

E = Effectively shut the concern out once and for all by using a summary closure statement, e.g., "So John, from what you've just said to me, it seems as though you are happy with that element of the product and how it will meet your objective of A, B, C... Are we OK to move ahead?" With luck, you'll then be able to move on to the next issue or, if possible, directly close the sale if the prospect appears satisfied that their biggest initial concern has been resolved.

This is an outline process only, but it's a combination of learning from many different sales resources and experiences... use it and see how you get along! If you apply it regularly and professionally, you'll definitely see those objections resolved more frequently and more comfortably! Enjoy the application!

Action Section

Visit www.businessbattleships.com and enter the username READER, with the password TARGET101 to access the online resources relevant to this chapter.

My 'hot' notes on this chapter

_____

_____

_____

_____

_____

_____

_____

_____

_____

_____

_____

_____

_____

The potential FEAR points my clients frequently raise objections about are:

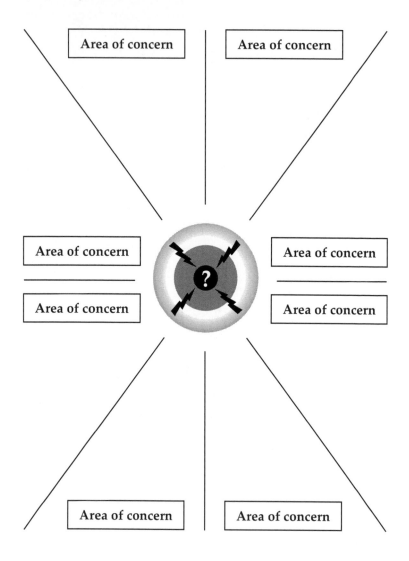

The best USP/ POD/guarantee/benefit statement I have to raise ahead of an objection being raised is:

For concern area 1:

For concern area 2:

For concern area 3:

For concern area 4:

For concern area 5:

For concern area 6:

For concern area 7:

For concern area 8:

Take out the objections before they even arise and you'll develop a stronger conversion through to sale!

CHAPTER 9

Have a process and bin
the no-entry signs

"A satisfied customer is the best business strategy of all"

Michael LeBoeuf

We've all had them. Those phone calls where the person on the other end of the line is very clearly following a script and has absolutely zero ability to switch back from robot repetition to human form.

Even worse: we've all experienced the 'dial one for another automated system, dial two for someone uninformed and uninterested, dial three to give up and return to the irritating music'.

Both of these experiences leave a sour taste in our mouth that simply says, "I'm never voluntarily engaging with this firm again."

Unfortunately, this kind of robotic approach to customer service is what people envisage when they say 'sales process'. In the following few pages I would like to state on record, "That is not what I mean."

So, what do I mean?

A sales process is simply a series of steps that remain human, remain responsive and remain value and client-focused.

All our effort in getting the prospect to the door shouldn't result in them arriving to a sign saying 'I'm not interested or indeed prepared'.

Preparation is key here and harking back to my military planning reference earlier, I'll use the Six Ps statement here:

'Prior planning and preparation prevents poor performance.'

Army proverb

The procedure we design for our sales process should be based around customer needs and wants, the delivery of an offer that reflects these needs and wants in terms of their gain and a simplicity to close that is not part of a customer prevention programme.

Sales processes vary from company to company, product to product and service to service, but the components of a good sales process are pretty consistent. This is where my revolving door principle comes in and I think you'll like it!

Imagine for a moment that every item you want to buy is housed in a different building on a street you're walking along. Welcome to 'Consumer Street'.

As you walk along the road, you identify the next purchase you may want to make and turn to face the front of the relevant building to consider the options on offer.

Imagine the front of that building has several sets of revolving doors through which you could potentially enter to make a purchase, but not all of them are open to you.

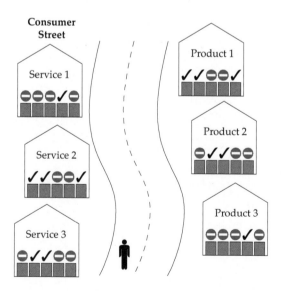

This is the situation in which our potential clients start off. The doors are a metaphor for each of the marketing channels by which we can reach and engage with them.

If we are not using a marketing approach that our potential client is able or willing to make use of, then this is the equivalent of placing a no-entry sign above a revolving door on the building. We are, in effect, closing off the very first door through which our prospect can progress towards a sale.

The essential point here is to identify the potential marketing channels and open as many of them as we can sensibly manage at any one time.

For example:

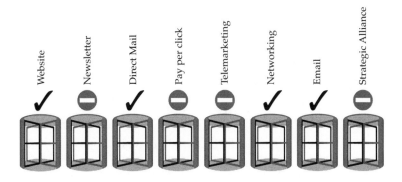

Once we have acted on this first recognition and taken the steps to open as many of the marketing doors as is feasible (the topic of this book up to now), then the next step is to decide on and plan the 'sales doors' that our customers will pass through on their way to paying for our future happiness!

An easy definition for where marketing ends and sales begin is to think of it in these terms:

Marketing: The doors that the prospect can see from 'Consumer Street'.

Sales: The series of doors that the prospect passes through once they have entered our building.

An example of how the number of 'sales doors' can differ for each marketing or product channel can be demonstrated by the situation in which someone is choosing to buy an item direct from a website.

The four door process:

Door 1 –   The ability to find the website through its online marketing, e.g. SEO, PPC, etc.

Door 2 –   The website itself. Is it interesting and easy for your customer to navigate through to what they want to buy?

Door 3 –   The item selection process. Is it easy to

place items into the shopping cart and then confirm the order?

Door 4 – The payment process. Is it easy to choose a payment method and then to transact?

Or there might be a two door option in response to a direct mail piece.

Door 1 – Did the letter get read and the message hit the mark in the first place?

Door 2 – When the prospect responded by telephoning to place an order, was it easy to transact with the other party?

These are just two options within the principle and it's worth remembering that more 'sales doors' does not necessarily mean a greater chance of the prospect not progressing. A sales door is something a prospect can easily pass through. A sales hurdle is something a prospect struggles to get past.

How many of the doors in your processes are in reality hurdles you have allowed to stay there that may trip up your prospects?

If there are too few doors, or too many hurdles in your transaction processes, it can be difficult to generate a sale at all!

Think about the value of the order and how much of a relationship is required to give confidence to the transaction. The number of stages (doors) will normally reflect this.

This means that a £5 transaction vs. a £5 million transaction will require a different level of detail and a different level of trust in most cases. It is therefore likely that a higher value sale will require a higher intensity sales process and, therefore, more doors!

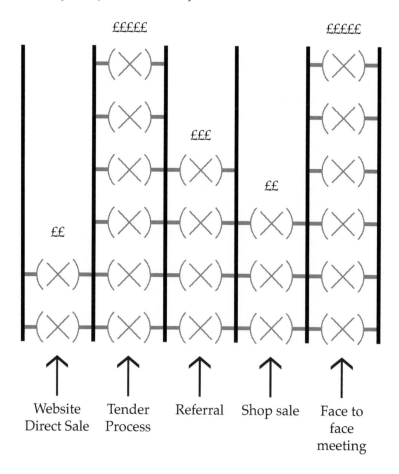

A 'sales door' here means a point of contact or customer engagement stage where there is the opportunity to further their progress in making a decision to buy. A sales hurdle simply encourages them to abandon their journey and dive out of the closest emergency exit back to 'Consumer Street'.

So... Three key questions to ask yourself about your company's marketing and sales processes right now, today, in the here and now, are:

1) How many potential **marketing doors** should your company now open that are currently showing the consumer a no-entry sign?

2) How many **sales doors** need to be built for each product or value type, to effectively build the trust and commitment required before sales can be made consistently?

3) How many of the current **sales hurdles/blockades** can you address and replace with a sales 'door' that the consumer can get past with your help?

Draft the doorways that exist in your own company process on a flipchart and highlight any areas where the process is a hurdle with a no-entry sign.

Then work on these areas in the near future and improve the buyer experience. It will affect the conversion rates and increase the number of clients that make it through to paying you!

The example below illustrates the task in action.

Stage 1 is simply the identification of buyer paths, sales doors and hurdles, e.g.:

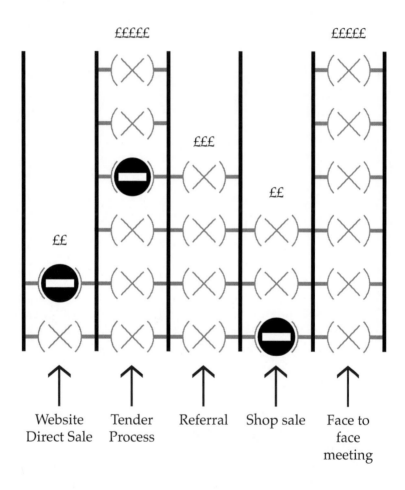

Stage 2 is working on the exact nature of the problem and board-blasting options to resolve them.

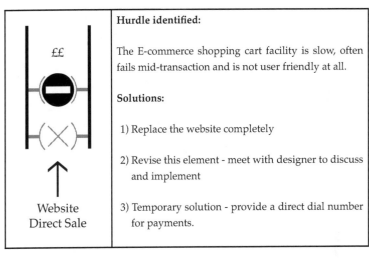

	Hurdle identified:
££	The E-commerce shopping cart facility is slow, often fails mid-transaction and is not user friendly at all.
	Solutions:
	1) Replace the website completely
	2) Revise this element - meet with designer to discuss and implement
Website Direct Sale	3) Temporary solution - provide a direct dial number for payments.

I'm willing to bet that right now you can already identify where a few hurdles exist! On the next page is a model that will help you stay accountable to delivering the necessary change.

Stage 3 is planning the improvements using a SMART goal basis

S à *Specific* =   *I will meet with Epsilon web design to identify costs, service interruption and options for a new shopping cart system. Once this is done, the correct solution will be implemented.*

M à *Measurable* =   *When clients use the new system, they will experience a faster transaction experience and a more consistent and reliable service. This will be tested every week for the first three months through in-house trial purchases.*

A à *Achievable* =	*This goal is achievable. There is sufficient operating cash available for a new IT project and budget for this has been allocated.*
R à *Result* =	*Repeat customer rate will improve, the number of complaints will decline and bounce rate will reduce. Reviewing the analytics on a weekly basis to check the status of start of process to sale made will assist in proving this. Secondary result will be higher turnover from this sales path.*
T à *Timeframe* =	*I will meet with Epsilon no later than 18th March and will have a full solution in place no later than 12th May.*

As you can see, once it's defined and planned there is little wriggle room in this goal-setting approach. All you need to do now is share that goal with whoever you choose to hold you accountable and decide what your reward and penalty should be.

Some of us are 'carrot' people; others are more 'stick' people.

If you know you respond better to reward, then set a goal that has a reward at the end. If you know you need the 'stick' to motivate you, then pick a penalty that has enough drive to make you complete the task!

As a final point in this chapter, I'd like to explain why I chose revolving doors as the analogy and add one extra point that can help you convince more clients to buy from you and to do it faster.

Revolving doors can take people forwards a step, or they can put them right back where they were a few moments ago. Not all actions you take in a sales process will move a person forwards, but they won't always cause a person to leave immediately either.

Within each revolving door is a series of segments and each of these can represent an objection handler for the process. In my experience, common objections can run through many stages of a sales process, but less common ones tend to appear at a particular point in time or during the process. For example, if we were selling cars it's unlikely that we would get a 'the ride is too firm' objection before the test drive phase of the sales process.

At this stage of the process, the car salesperson would need to identify the correct segment of the next revolving door to encourage the prospect to move on a stage.

For example:

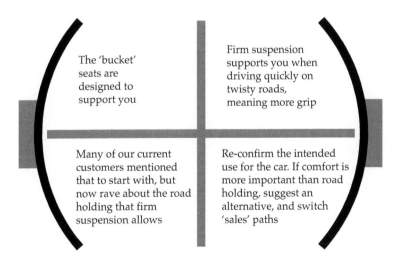

This is a fictional example, but it demonstrates that having potential objection handlers identified and prepared for each stage can help to move customers effectively and efficiently through the sales doors and prevent a block point from forming.

Summary

FIRST

Identify the marketing doors your prospects can see are 'open for business' from 'Consumer Street'…

THEN

Identify the sales paths that exist and the number of doors for each route the prospect may take…

THEN

Review the current doors to ensure they are easy to go through. Where you find a hurdle in the place of a doorway, do a bit of business DIY.

AND FINALLY

Use pre-objection handlers for each phase that will enable your sales team to either progress prospects to the next stage, or effectively translate objections to a suitable sales path to suit their needs and wishes.

Action Section

Visit www.businessbattleships.com and enter the username READER, with the password TARGET101 to access the online resources relevant to this chapter.

My 'hot' notes on this chapter

The doors of my company that are visible from 'Consumer Street':

e.g., my website, telemarketing, a Facebook page, street signage, etc.

1 _____

2 _____

3 _____

4 _____

5 _____

6 _____

7 _____

8 _____

9 _____

10 _____

Among the doorways my prospects can see from 'Consumer Street', I have reviewed my processes and can identify the following are effective at all stages:

For those that have a doorway, but have sales hurdles or no-entry signs posted, detail the stages that need to be adjusted or enhanced to enable an effective sales transit to take place.

Hurdle Identified	Potential solutions to improve the situation

CHAPTER 10

Ask great questions and listen!

"The Art of a great question doesn't lie in the question itself, but in how much the recipient invests in their response."

Tim Rylatt

Focus your prospect's attention and take them from 'YOU and US' through to 'WE'

Your audience probably have their brain filters directed on to something entirely different. They are open to hearing from you, but right at this moment in time something else is the subject of their immediate tunnel vision. Maybe it's dinner. Maybe it's the attractive brunette sitting in the office next door. Maybe it's the pile of work they have sitting in front of them right now. Whatever it is, you need to get them to swing their attention spotlight on to the space your offering is occupying.

The second element in this principle is the need to take out the **fictional barrier** that exists in sales – this being the opinion that there is one party gaining, while the other party is paying for their gain. Typically, the view is that the salesperson is engaged in a contest of wills against the buyer and that is demonstrated in the following two statements:

Salesperson: I get this sale, I get a commission and that's the only way I will be satisfied here.

Buyer: He gets his sale and I am out of pocket, but don't really gain anything.

This perception is actually a complete myth of what SHOULD be happening if your sales team is doing it right. I love the title of Cassara's book *From Selling to Serving* as it sums up the real aim of a great salesperson.

Why?

Because any great salesperson today knows that a commission earned through 'selling' rather than 'helping the customer' is destined to be the only sale they will ever make to that person. Buyers begrudge being sold something they haven't actually chosen to buy.

A true salesperson has the ability to guide the prospect through the process of value recognition effectively. And they will do that in such a way that it addresses the prospect's genuine concerns and desires, to help them make their own decision in a manner that relates to the genuine benefits and outcomes they can experience through the salesperson's product or service.

Help your target audience focus on the offering you want them to and view this challenge as a project that can be completed by using a series of well-composed questions.

Here's how to do that:

Use open questions.

Questions that make them THINK about the product or service and to which their answer will give you some more information to work with.

WHO

WHAT

WHEN

WHERE

WHY

HOW

These are all 'lead in' words for an open question and should provide an answer that is more detailed than 'yes' or 'no'.

Once you've got one answer, use more open questions to draw out emotion from it. For example, the conversation below which is between a salesperson and a buyer.

The salesperson is asking the questions here and is working for a premier parcel delivery firm. The buyer runs a mail order company and currently uses a different delivery firm to manage their despatches.

The conversation below is a simple transcript and shows the flow of communication between both parties. In this example, it's fairly obvious that the sales process is poor. But I'd like to make a point and ask you the question: "Have you ever found yourself in 'tell' mode?" I have… and this is the result.

Q.   So, you obviously use a delivery firm today, but I'm here to tell you why you want to change. We offer a good rate, own 100 vans and two ships and we have a really strong record in working with companies across the globe. We can deliver all your parcels to the local area as well as internationally and I have a form here that you can sign to get started. Would you like to change?

A.   **No!**

Here's how the conversation could be handled more effectively. Switch to focus question mode.

Q.   What is the most common concern that you have when it comes to delivering your items to your clients and where is that showing most in the experience they get?

A.   We've had some difficulties in ensuring the parcels that we despatch on time actually arrive on time, as a result of inconsistency beyond our control in the company we have been using to deliver the items to our clients.

Q.   Hmmm, that sounds like it could be a real problem… How do you feel about that?

A.   It's a real pain and is making me really stressed.

Q.   That's no good then, is it? What is the response you're getting from your customers about that situation?

A.   It has a big impact on their perception of us. It's unfair, but I know we have lost customers because of the delivery company's mistakes.

Q.   Wow, from what you have said that seems like an issue that you really need fixed quickly. How long have you been suffering with this stressful situation?

A.   Ages... but I haven't been able to find anything better at a sensible cost. I really want to change things.

Q.   Well, that sounds like it's been building up and up for a while and is now really frustrating for you. I do think there is some light at the end of the tunnel though, and have some ideas that would certainly help with getting your clients to stay, through enabling you a more consistent delivery method. How would you feel if we could work together on coming up with some potential solutions to that problem?

A. **OK, that sounds like it's worth exploring.**

MUCH better, isn't it?

Here's why it proves so much more effective...

I have repeated this conversation again below and have identified within it the purpose of choosing particular words or a particular questioning style. This will help you recognise why they prove more effective and draws out the main elements that will help you to use these ideas in your own sales engagements:

Q.   What is the most common concern that you have when it comes to delivering your items to your clients and where is that showing most in the experience they get?

THIS QUESTION DRAWS THE FOCUS ON TO PRODUCT DELIVERY AND THEREFORE THE OFFERING OF OUR COMPANY.

A.   We've had some difficulties in ensuring the parcels that we despatch on time actually arrive on time, as a result of inconsistency beyond our control in the company we have been using to deliver the items to our clients.

Q.   Hmmm, that sounds like it could be a real problem... how do you feel about that?

THE PROSPECT REPLIED BASED ON LOGIC AND A COGNITIVE ASSESSMENT OF WHAT THE FACTS WERE, LEADING TO AN ISSUE. AS A SALESPERSON, I NEED TO REACH EMOTION IN THEM TO BACK UP A LOGIC-BASED CHOICE. BUYING DECISIONS ARE BASED ON EMOTION MORE OFTEN THAN LOGIC ALONE.

A.   It's a real pain and is making me really stressed.

Q.   That's no good then, is it? What is the response you're getting from your customers about that situation?

I'VE ALREADY FOUND OUT ABOUT THEIR PERSONAL EMOTION, BUT NOW I'M TRYING TO LEVERAGE THAT FRUSTRATION BY HIGHLIGHTING THE KNOCK-ON EFFECTS OF THE SITUATION. BY IDENTIFYING THE SHARED ANNOYANCE OF THEIR FIRM AND THEIR CLIENTS, IT BECOMES AN ISSUE THEY HAVE TO DEAL WITH.

A.   It has a big impact on their perception of us. It's unfair, but I know we have lost customers because of the delivery company's mistakes.

Q.   Wow, from what you have said, that seems like an issue that you really need fixed quickly. How long have you been suffering with this stressful situation?

THIS QUESTION IS DESIGNED TO HELP THEM RECOGNISE THAT THERE IS A DEGREE OF URGENCY IN ADDRESSING THE TOPIC. BY GETTING THEM TO REALISE THAT THEY ARE NOT IN A COMFORTABLE PLACE AND IT'S ONLY GETTING WORSE WITH TIME, THEY ARE DRIVEN THROUGH EMOTION AND LOGIC TO A POINT OF WANTING TO MAKE A CHANGE.

A.   Ages... but I haven't been able to find anything better at anything like a sensible cost. I really want to change things.

Q. Well, that sounds like it's been building up and up for a while and is now really frustrating for you. I do think there is some light at the end of the tunnel though, and have some ideas that would certainly help out with getting your clients to stay, through enabling you a more consistent delivery method. How would you feel if we could work together on coming up with some potential solutions to that problem?

THE FIRST PART IS CONFIRMING BACK TO THEM THAT THIS IS A MAGNIFYING ISSUE. THE LONGER YOU LEAVE IT, THE WORSE IT GETS. USING THIS TOPIC OF URGENCY, THE SECOND PART IS BUILDING IN THEIR MIND THE PICTURE OF A MORE POSITIVE FUTURE FOR THEM, IN THE CONTEXT OF WORKING WITH ME. THE FINAL PART IS HELPING THEM BRIDGE THE GAP BETWEEN THEM AND US – CREATING A 'WE' APPROACH. THIS IS IMPORTANT AS IT TAKES AWAY THE FICTIONAL BARRIER AND MAKES ME ONE OF THEIR TEAM WORKING ON 'OUR' PROJECT AND SHARING A POSITIVE COMMON OBJECTIVE TO DELIVER THINGS ON TIME TO 'OUR CUSTOMERS'.

A. OK, that sounds like it's worth exploring.

FOCUS their attention and get their brain filters aligned with your offering and you'll get a much higher level of both engagement and conversion to sale. This mock conversation shows one approach.

Helping them remember the future can feel better

The audience is waiting to show interest in your product or service. All they need is the right reason. Thinking back to the connection between left and right brain, give some thought to which open questions you can ask in a given situation, to make the prospect mentally picture themselves, a person, or a company in a given scenario.

For example:

If you were selling a sun cream of which the USP was that it was quickly absorbed into the skin, you might use a starter question like: "So John, this summer when you take your kids to the beach on a hot day, what are some of the biggest frustrations you'll experience in making sure they are protected from the sun?"

This question serves two purposes. Firstly, it encourages the prospect to picture themselves in a situation that is familiar (right brain creative imagery).

Secondly, it generates an emotional recognition in the brain associated with the task they have to complete.

In the previous section, I referred to the common sales error of 'telling your prospect' why they should buy. Understanding how our left and right brain works, and translating this into effective questioning that will help your prospect put themselves into the mental picture you draw for them, takes the sales decision process away from being based purely on logic or your own reasons for them to accept your sale. It drives their brain to use the right side. When they picture a given situation in their mind and they imagine what it feels like to be living that scenario, then something truly impressive takes place...

They actually experience that scenario in a way that is indistinguishable from a genuine memory.

I know that sounds odd, but it's a fact that your brain cannot distinguish an emotion experienced within a real situation from a perceived emotion experienced within an imaginary situation. This may be one of the fundamental reasons why cognitive behavioural therapy and hypnosis are so widely used to manage situations where there is an emotional change desired by a patient.

Think about it this way: lots of people have a fear of spiders and many of those same people will find it difficult to shift their perception of how a spider can be anything other than terrifying. However, when a person who has held an emotional fear of spiders has a positive experience involving a spider (whatever that may be!), then their future perception of what it would be like to meet one will be adjusted.

Using this principle doesn't mean you'll magically adjust a strong fear, but encouraging the prospect to picture themselves in a scenario where they are experiencing a positive result from your product or service can help to reduce the emotional barrier that can prevent a sale from being made.

To fully achieve this, the lead-in to creating that mental image needs to be convincing enough that they can actually visualise the scenario. This is easy for some people and harder for others, but your skill in weaving that imaginary paintbrush is where this will start to pay off. If you've ever been asked to deliberately NOT think about a pink elephant, you'll recognise the graphic creation power the brain has!

By using a series of simple questions to gauge a person's experience and to help them 'remember' their experience from the past, you can paint a vision of the future which will facilitate the process. Taking the same product as before, here's an example of how that can be achieved:

Q. "Paul, where did you last go to the beach with your family?"

A. "In Florida."

Q. "Sounds great! What was it like there?"

A. "Wonderful. Hot weather, swaying palms and the whitest sand you've ever seen!"

Q. "That sounds fantastic. What did you enjoy doing most while you were there?"

A. "Well, our kids loved playing in the sea and my wife and I enjoyed relaxing in the sun for a few days."

Q. "Well, relaxing in the sun while your kids play at the water's edge does sound amazing. I bet you can picture that in your mind right now!"

A. "Yes I can."

Q. "So tell me Paul, while you were on that beach in Florida, did you experience any frustrations when trying to get your kids to put their sun cream on regularly throughout the day?"

A. "Absolutely! The kids hated the greasiness of the cream and I remember them getting annoyed with myself and my wife for 'nagging' them. They avoided putting cream on at all whenever they could."

Q. "Sounds like a frustrating challenge and one your kids found irritating too! So, I just want you to imagine for a moment you are sitting back on that beach and you've just asked the kids to put their sun cream on. This time, though, you have a product that is just as protective, but is absorbed quickly and easily into the skin. Do you feel like that would be an improvement worth making?"

A.   "For sure. Anything that could get them back to enjoying the sun and sea so I can get back to relaxing gets my vote!"

Q.   "Great. Based on what you've told me, we have the perfect product so you can you bin that irritating greasy cream and keep your kids safe and happy, while also letting you relax!"

This solid reaffirmation of a changed emotional experience, either based on a past real experience or one that is sufficiently real through visualisation, is an interesting and fun sales technique to try and use!

Please note: If you are still sitting on the sceptic fence on this strategy (and I can understand why you might be, because it's a little more 'out there' than some of the more general approaches), then I encourage you to do a little research on a book called *Psycho-cybernetics* by Dr. Maxwell Maltz. Maltz worked in the field of psychology and specifically focused on the power of positive affirmation in belief systems. He specialised in the treatment of patients who had suffered from disfigurement and underwent facial plastic surgery. To address the challenge in which patients had a distorted perception of how they would be perceived by others, and indeed would perceive themselves as a result, he encouraged the patients to practise positive affirmations and to visualise themselves in a positive frame, but with an underlying sense of realism. In this section of the book, I have linked the findings of Maltz (that an emotive visualisation can impact a belief system about oneself) with the idea that personal valuation of self or surroundings is directly linked to the likelihood of a prospect becoming a buyer through that same valuation filter. The primary shift is taking the principles from the visualising exercises he used with plastic surgery patients and using them within a sales arena.

Just like the patient holds a value of self that can be adjusted through positive visualisation and hypnotic reaffirmation, the client you deal with has an expectation of an outcome they will experience through your product or service. The technique is therefore applicable and I have found its application has definite impact in achieving a shift in perception prior to the buying decision being made or not. This matches the sales principles used in so many business training books and materials, of finding the pain a prospect is experiencing in the here and now and then using questions to drive their desire for a better future. What I suggest here is to take that idea and to really use it to encourage the prospect to visualise themselves using your service or product and associate the emotional response they would attain by doing so.

It might interest you to know that Zig Ziglar, Brian Tracy and Tony Robbins have also used some of these same principles in their approaches to self-help books and the building of confidence within salespeople! If it works for the salesperson to develop their confidence in the success of their own actions, then the same must be true for buyers, if we can help them practise it subconsciously. After all, salespeople themselves are in fact often the customers of others outside of the workplace!

Action Section

Visit www.businessbattleships.com and enter the username READER, with the password TARGET101 to access the online resources relevant to this chapter.

My 'hot' notes on this chapter

CHAPTER 11

Today's buyers are tank commanders

"As a person becomes more and more defensive, he becomes less able to perceive accurately the motives, values and emotions of the sender."

Jack Gibb

In the last two chapters, we've got a little bit more scientific in our approach to conversion rate and how to make our buyers react the way we want them to.

All valid stuff and, if used well, highly effective in moving a person from one viewpoint on a topic to another. But I feel it's a good time to take stock of the situation and gain a big picture perspective.

I watched Dr. Ivan Misner (the founder of BNI networking groups) deliver a presentation in Miami this year and picked up on a crucial point that is pertinent to this stage in my book.

I'll admit it, I expected Dr. Misner to use his presentation as a pitch for BNI and to wax lyrical about the benefits of networking. Now there's no doubting that he's a proactive exponent for the strategy, or indeed that he holds a strong belief that it's a very effective marketing means. (I agree with him on both counts by the way!)

The thing is, Dr. Misner caught me off-guard during his presentation. You see, I'd expected one approach and received something totally different. Where I had expected a lecture, I received guidance from a friend. Where I expected this prominent and successful leader to present and run, he stayed and talked. When getting a book signed by him, I expected the statutory handshake smile and "NEXT" call, but in fact received some personally relevant advice and a friendly first-name chat.

Not particularly significant as stories go, you may be thinking, but in fact it brought home to me a reality about the sales and marketing profession. The reality being that ALL of us, myself included, have become a little expectant and a little cynical.

We've become masters of wariness and cautious of what's on offer at every stage and in every environment. Perhaps a little too cautious and cynical for our own good. Thank you Dr. Misner for helping me recognise this trait within myself.

The following few pages detail how that learning HAS helped me and hopefully WILL help you engage more easily with your prospects.

How does all this relate to tank commanders? Ah, well that bit is easy to explain...

Pretty much since birth we've been subjected to marketing and sales of one form or another. We've become so expert at managing it that we barely notice when it's happening to us.

So expert that we have our automatic defences in place, and so expert that we don't even hear the defensive guns going off when we fire them!

Many everyday situations demonstrate this.

When you pass a bus shelter and see the advert telling you that lunch is just 100 metres away and available for a bargain price. The simple fact that you don't walk there every single time you feel the slightest pang of hunger proves the point.

The knock-back you provide to the door-to-door window salesman.

The polite refusal of an invitation to dance.

And so on and so on and so on.

Every time you've said 'no' to an offering, you've been using these defences, even when you didn't say a word but acted in a way that took you away from giving in. You were using your defences.

Here's the thing...

As a consumer we HAVE to use our defences. If we didn't, we'd be really broke really quickly and own a whole load of products and services we neither need nor really want.

Going back to our brain filter learning from earlier on in this book, we only pay attention to a small fraction of what's being offered to us, and even when we do our defences are so honed that the marketer or salesperson has to work their socks off to get anywhere near to a "Yes please, that sounds great!"

We are all, in fact, tank commanders. We've got a hulking great set of armour around us that is pretty much impenetrable and a paranoid reflexive behaviour that means that the vast majority get told 'no', for no better reason than survival. I'd actually go so far as to say that we've battened down all the hatches, switched on all the surveillance gadgetry available to us and have a hostile attitude to anything and everything around us that we haven't previously trialled and proven harmless.

Hatch... only used in safe environment or times of dire trouble!

Main Gun... used to ward off poor sales people

Blind-spot... used to ignore irrelevant or poor marketing campaigns!

Tracks... used to run away at the first sign of unwanted selling

So, as a marketer or salesperson, we ideally need to stop asking the really difficult questions:

"How do I get to the person inside that tank? How can I blow that armour off until they have to give in to me?"

No, what we need to do is get better at asking a different question entirely:

"How can I convince the terrified person inside that tank that it's a safe environment and, in fact, I'm not the enemy but an ally?"

Master that one and you'll get more than just the single sale; you'll get clients that will work with you on common aims.

It won't be 'them and us', it will be just 'us'.

This is particularly challenging in industries that carry a poor reputation, or for which the majority of consumers are naturally suspicious.

Personally, I find this is the case when dealing with things and people that are highly technical. It's not that I don't trust in general; I just struggle to trust something I don't really understand – and I suspect I'm not alone in that!

GREAT! We now know that for all our skill in sales and marketing, it really comes down to trust and clarity. What do I now do with that knowledge?

Use it to answer the three questions that your prospects are always asking:

1) **"Who is this company... what level of faith do I hold in them?"**

2) **"If I haven't yet tried or experienced the product/ service, how can I be assured about my decision?"**

And most important of all...

3) **"Can I trust you, the salesperson, who has a vested interest in relieving me of my money... but is there more than that in what you say and do?"**

Work on some ideas to blend your sales and marketing strategies with messages that effectively communicate a positive answer to these three crucial questions and you'll be well on the path to business glory!

Action Section

Visit www.businessbattleships.com and enter the username READER, with the password TARGET101 to access the online resources relevant to this chapter.

My 'hot' notes on this chapter

Write a short paragraph detailing how the customer will describe their experience when you are the professional, knowledgeable, efficient and effective ally HELPING THEM TO BUY.

Below, list the top three habits you know you have that make customers back off from making a purchase from you personally. *(This means being really honest about your personal skill-set, mindset and behaviour during sales activity.)*

1 _____

_____

_____

_____

2 _____

_____

_____

_____

3 _____

_____

_____

_____

To ensure you become and are seen to be a genuine ally in your customers' buying process and experience, what are the three essential behaviours that you will adopt from today onwards that will create a 'safer' buying environment for them when holding sales meetings / calls?

1 _____

_____

_____

2 _____

_____

_____

3 _____

_____

_____

_____

CHAPTER 12

The art of presentation

"To teach is to learn twice"

Joseph Joubert

Taking on board the final words of the last chapter, if we want to win our audience on to our team, then we'd better not only have a compelling case, but an effective method of delivering it too.

For those of you engaged in sales, this usually means ensuring that your presentation skills are up to scratch. Whether you're delivering the pitch in person, via email or over the phone, there are several tricks of the trade that will help you really nail your presentations.

First amongst these tips is to remember the key point…

There is no perfect system.

In this chapter, I'll give you suggestions and share some things that I've learned from several years of presenting, both in sales and in education. They are not RULES and I have generally found that the very best presentations I've seen have stepped outside the boundaries and delivered something above and beyond. So don't read this section of the book and think, 'That's it, the only way to do it'. You'll limit your capability that way, so I'd like you to add to my suggestions using your own creative mind.

1. Have a structure!

Off the cuff presentations can be OK, but in my experience the well-prepared tend to win the day. Have a structure that both you and the prospect can work to. This is almost always preceded by explaining this process to the prospect in advance of actually delivering it. Why? Well, most of us dislike not knowing what to expect. It's not that you can't add to a planned presentation (in fact I'd encourage that), but it helps to have an outline to work to.

If you take this principle and use it well, you can pre-handle objections by covering the topic during the presentation. You can also pre-suggest the situation of the prospect making a positive decision at the end of the presentation.

When the presentation lacks a structure and the prospect finds themselves unexpectedly having to take action, then the sales process breaks down. Let them know it's coming. They can then gauge what you are saying against their own expectation and value set. By the time you reach the close, you'll already have them in the mindset of decision-making. Whether it's 'yes', 'no' or 'I have a few questions', they know what's expected and the classic 'I'd like to think it over' is less likely to feature.

2. Appeal to all three learning domains

Your audience has a natural preference to learn one of three ways: visually, via audio, or through physical involvement. In the educational world, VAK testing (visual, auditory, kinaesthetic) is an easy way of finding preferences. But more than likely you won't have the benefit of a report on which to base your presentation style, so it's best to include all three preferences where possible.

This can be achieved by using a blend of visual stimuli, well-chosen and delivered speech or music and, where feasible, the opportunity for the audience to engage physically with the product or situation.

3. Be professional!

Easy to forget in the heat of the moment but remember that, right from the word go, you are representing yourself, the company and the product or service. The way you handle the presentation and any other element of your marketing and sales process must be consistent with the perception you want your client to have of you.

The materials and language you use in your presentation are important and should be designed to develop trust in the three areas that really matter: trust in you, trust in the product/service and trust in the company.

If the product or service requires the prospect to be confident in their own capability to use it, then the fourth dimension of 'trust in themselves' becomes important. This final element of trust is particularly important when your audience lacks technical know-how or understanding, but perceives that is what is required for a successful buyer experience. Examples of this would be the sale of a laptop or IT service to the elderly, or financial advisory services to an individual with poor current knowledge of investments.

In both situations, the prospect knows they have a need for the product or service, but the company that offers the easiest engagement and simplest use of language is likely to win the sale. I've found this to be particularly true in the field of business coaching, where it's often not just the highbrow level of knowledge of the coach that wins the client's confidence, but also their ability to explain concepts clearly and support clients. In other words, the client will often trust the coach and their company, but doubt their own ability to use the expertise and skill-set they are learning from them.

4. Use THEIR language

One of the most common errors in a presentation (especially in sales) is the use of jargon or personal language. Your familiarity with your own process, service or product may well be your downfall. When delivering your presentation, imagine you're engaging with your own product or service for the very first time and put yourself squarely in the client's mindset. Identify their concerns, manage their fears and use their language to explain things through.

As an experienced 'customer', we all know the frustration of speaking to 'geek-boy'. That's the person who cannot speak our language but clearly knows his own REALLY well. The frustration they experience in getting concepts across, coupled with the prospect's embarrassment at acknowledging their 'ignorance', is a recipe for disaster!

Ditch the jargon and speak your audience's language to stand a better chance of success. As a small caution here: when you're pitching to peers and other experts use language that is consistent with them.

A simple model that brought this home to me was one I learned when training for police suspect interviews.

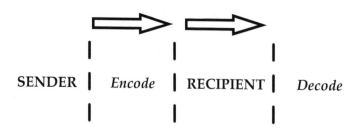

SENDER | *Encode* | RECIPIENT | *Decode*

This diagram shows the way in which communication occurs. When we start talking, we 'encode' our message using our language, tonality, body language, etc.

Our audience (or recipient) receives our communication and then their brain decodes the meaning.

The key point is that there are actually not one, but two opportunities for the messages to get screwed up – at our end as the sender, or their end as the recipient. Whether we intend it or not, one of these avenues is always open!

Here's how you can minimise the chance of miscommunication: the more you use the language and referencing points of your audience, the less likely it becomes that this error will occur, because you're ensuring the encoding is more consistent with the decoding.

5. Summarise key points

You'll almost certainly either have seen legal drama shows, attended a genuine courtroom hearing, or possibly even engaged in one yourself!

One thing that is really obvious (when you know to look for it) is the use of repetition in an effective presentation. All great presenters and many professional salespeople have learned that listening attentively to the audience and repeating back the key phrases or words and ideas they provide is crucial to fully engaging with them.

In the mock conversation below, you'll see this in action:

"So tell me Dan, what is it that frustrates you about your current gym programme?"

"Well, I find that doing the stepper every time is really boring and my legs hurt for days afterwards."

"Hmmm, that sounds painful. Your legs hurt for days afterwards, you say?"

"Yes, absolutely."

"Dan, having heard how boring you say the stepper is and knowing how hurtful that process is proving, how would you feel about trialling a different means of strengthening your legs?"

It's only a short conversation, but there are several uses of the client's language. The alternative would be where the personal trainer provides these answers instead…

"So tell me Dan, what is it that frustrates you about your current gym programme?"

"Well, I find that doing the stepper every time is really boring and my legs hurt for days afterwards."

"OK, so you're getting too much lactic acid building in your quadriceps?"

"Yes, I guess."

"Dan, we need to review your metabolic process management and identify a more productive muscle mass generating system. Are you up for that?"

"I really don't know, that sounds a bit complex for me. I'm after something a bit less challenging."

The second example is 'geek-boy working overtime', if you catch my drift. If you want a positive and emotionally engaging communication with a positive, common goal outcome, use simple language, your audience's vocabulary and make sure you repeat back the salient points. That way they'll know you listened to, recognised and valued what they had to say.

Try the idea of repetition and summary using your prospect's language in a sales environment; you might just like the results it brings you!

6. Be gracious in defeat, but learn from it so that it doesn't become your habit and 'go-to place'

Be warned: Sometimes you won't win the sale... even knowing what you now know.

Your parents may have said to you in the past, "Never mind, it's the taking part that counts." But in this case that isn't entirely true; the taking part is only the very beginning. The more you take part, however, the better your chances of becoming an expert in the field, so get out there and practise your socks off.

Because:

The one overriding factor that will prove definitive in making a lasting and significant change to your marketing and sales success is this...

BE PREPARED TO LISTEN AND ADAPT

This is actually much easier said than done and I have heard (and said!) many times before "It wasn't my fault"; "They moved the goalposts"; "They didn't really know what they wanted" etc., etc.

None of these reasons helped me progress or grow!

The excuses list is long and distinguished for all of us, but the truth tends to be much less convoluted and much simpler. The challenge lies in being willing to look for the simple truth, rather than creating an easy lie.

If a 'client' said 'no' but they did fit the right profile and had a genuine need for our service or product, then the only person we can blame is ourselves. It really is that simple.

Something we did or didn't do, say, act upon or listen to caused the reaction in them to say 'no'. We can blame them or other factors, but it doesn't turn back time. And crucially, it doesn't change their mind or the decision of a future similar prospect, until *you* change.

So learning to listen, reflect and refine our approach is the only sure-fire way for any of us to improve and develop.

DON'T let yourself off the hook by giving into weak character traits or making up excuses.

DO ask for help and review, record, or practise with another professional. Even as a business coach, I can say that none of us can view our own performance completely objectively, even if our intention is good. We can only ever see it from our own viewpoint, using the education upon which that is based. If you want to excel, getting a second opinion and insight from another pair of eyes is as important in business as it is in sports or any other field of endeavour.

The person who said 'no' represents a chance to improve. It represents an opportunity that is tapping you on the shoulder and drawing your attention to the chance to be better next time. And what a boring world we'd live in if there was never a chance to develop like this?

If you view NO as the enemy, then you are destined to repeat mistakes and you'll only ever go so far. Look at it with an open mind and a self-critical appraising eye and perhaps engage someone else's eyes to do the same. Do this and the world's your oyster. The steps to YES will become that much clearer to see and your ability to move up them will become that much simpler.

Action Section

Visit www.businessbattleships.com and enter the username READER, with the password TARGET101 to access the online resources relevant to this chapter.

My 'hot' notes on this chapter

In summary

I trust you have found learning the ideas and approaches in this book an eye-opening experience.

My intention with it was to enable as many of you as possible to reach your sales and marketing potential and to make the experience of being a customer of yours enjoyable and memorable! I wanted to provide a different business book that takes a fresh approach to the topics for which there are endless sources of advice.

If you found this to be a little different – good.

If you plan on using some of the ideas and if this book challenged some of your sales and marketing preconceptions – even better.

Let me know how you get along. I'd be delighted to hear of your successes using the ideas represented here!

Tim Rylatt

About the author

Tim Rylatt is a multi-award winning business coach based in Haywards Heath, West Sussex, England.

He was born and raised in Worthing, enjoys sea fishing and motorcycling during his spare time and has a fantastic supportive wife, Juliet.

Tim started his career working as an Operational Front Line Officer for Sussex Police and undertook a variety of specialist roles, before moving to The States of Guernsey Police. While in the Channel Islands, Tim qualified as a Training Officer and was involved in the development of the island's first locally delivered two-year training programme.

Following a serious knee injury sustained while playing hockey, Tim's frontline police career was curtailed and he moved back to Sussex. Here, during recent years, he has built and runs a successful business coaching firm with Juliet, as part of the ActionCOACH network.

Tim has helped hundreds of business owners each year to understand the key principles behind sustainable business growth and holds a strong personal interest in the underlying reasons that consumers choose to buy or not. It is this interest that led him to write Business Battleships and the intention remains to write several more titles on different business topics in the coming years. So watch this space!

If you'd like to contact Tim about this book or about involving him as a coach or speaker for your organisation, he can be reached via the 'contact the author' link on www.businessbattleships.com.

"The educated differ from the uneducated as much as the living from the dead."

Aristotle

2234626R00107

Printed in Great Britain
by Amazon.co.uk, Ltd.,
Marston Gate.